MW00326105

A BLACK
REVOLUTIONARY'S
LIFE IN LABOR

A BLACK REVOLUTIONARY'S LIFE IN LABOR:

BLACK WORKERS POWER IN DETROIT

MICHAEL HAMLIN *with* **MICHELE GIBBS**

A BLACK REVOLUTIONARY'S LIFE IN LABOR:
Black Workers Power in Detroit

First printing: From the Field, Oaxaca, Mexico, 2012.
Second printing: Against the Tide Books,
Personal Histories in the Struggle for Justice,
Detroit, Michigan, 2013.
P.O. Box 44793, Detroit, MI 48244
mikechamlin@gmail.com

Cover design by: Christina Hamlin
Cover photographs: Courtesy of General Baker
Page design by: *www.wordzworth.com*

Genre: Historical Narrative

Black History · Black Workers · History of Black Working Class
· Black Power – Detroit, Michigan – American History &
Sociology – Black Studies – Afro-American History –
Community Organizing

ISBN: 978-0-615-71813-2

Credits: In-plant newsletter "Speak Out" July 1967 issue from
Michele Gibbs Collection. Collages and artwork by Michele
Gibbs. DRUM Slate poster photo and DRUM Programmatic
Demands, courtesy of General Baker. Photo Gallery from the
film "Finally Got the News" printed with permission from Rene
Lichtman and Stu Bird of California Newsreel. Poem by Dudley
Randall printed with permission from the Dudley Randall
Estate. Retirement dinner photos by Frank Hammer.

CONTENTS

A BLACK REVOLUTIONARY'S LIFE IN LABOR: BLACK WORKERS POWER IN DETROIT

Michael Hamlin   Michele Gibbs

In 2011, almost half a century after the struggles of the sixties and the founding of the League of Revolutionary Black Workers, Michele Gibbs initiated a series of conversations with Mike Hamlin in order to obtain, record and make public his reflections on the struggles for a more just social order to which both have been committed throughout their lives, "A Black Revolutionary's Life in Labor" brings us Hamlin's important thoughts on the social justice movement's past and possible future.

From the introduction by George Colman.

This book is dedicated to my brother,
my comrade, my friend, Michael Hamlin,
who kept his head while all about him
were losing theirs, and blaming it on him.
En la lucha, siempre, con amor.

—MICHELE GIBBS

INTRODUCTION

by George D. Colman

I am one of the many who are grateful for the life and work of Michael Hamlin. Mike and I have known each other over the long years since the 1960's when he, a young, black revolutionary reached out to contact, inform and involve white men and women in the struggle for social justice in Detroit. I was then a young clergyman on the staff of the Presbyterian Church working closely with representatives of other Protestant denominations, the Roman Catholic Church and the Detroit Council of Churches in the work against racism, poverty and powerlessness in the city and the war in Vietnam abroad. And for all of us, the thought and action of black leaders like Mike Hamlin and Ken Cockrel provided important guidance.

As the text of Michele Gibbs' new and important book, *A Black Revolutionary's Life in Labor* makes clear, Hamlin influenced the thought and work of many of us not only through his numerous personal contacts but even more through the creation of organizations like the Control Conflict and Change book club in which over 300 men and women met regularly to discuss presentations and readings representing a variety of political interpretations and approaches to social change.

Michael Hamlin, the son of Mississippi sharecroppers, a Korean war veteran, University of Michigan student and truck driver for the Detroit News was a key organizer and leader of the League of Revolutionary Black Workers, a life-time friend and resource for black workers in the unions and factories of Motown from the early 1960's through the first decade of the 21st century.

Hamlin and Gibbs have known each other, worked together, been friends and allies for more than forty years. He was prominent among those who encouraged Michele Gibbs to move to Detroit and become part of the leadership of the recently formed League of Revolutionary Black Workers in the late 1960's because of her well known work as a committed intellectual, writer and educator, her history as a SNCC activist and her experience as an anti-Vietnam War Movement Veteran throughout the sixties.

It was also Mike Hamlin who called me one early morning in 1971 at the Detroit Industrial Mission, an organization working against racism and sexism in Detroit corporations and suggested we interview Michele Gibbs Russell for the staff position then open. We did interview her, were grateful for the recommendation and Michele began her work with DIM almost immediately. Our work together as a team formed the basis of a partnership for life.

In 2011, almost half a century after the struggles of the sixties and the founding of the League of Revolutionary Black Workers, Gibbs initiated a series of conversations with Hamlin in order to obtain, record and make public his reflections on the struggles for a more just social order to which both have been committed throughout their lives. *A Black Revolutionary's Life in Labor* brings us Hamlin's important thoughts on the social justice movement's past and possible future.

In the history of the left in the United States, Mike Hamlin first came to public attention as one of the important organizers of the League of Revolutionary Black Workers in Detroit, an organization that captured national attention in the late sixties and early seventies. The historian Manning Marable claimed the League was "in many respects the most significant expression of black radical thought and activism in the 1960's".

And James Geschwender in his book *Class, Race, and Worker Insurgency* summarized a part of the League's significant history with these words, "The League of Revolutionary Black Workers... first appeared on the Detroit scene in 1968 when the Dodge Revolutionary Union Movement (DRUM) was formed... The League during its brief existence organized black workers, conducted demonstrations, held wildcat strikes, participated in union electoral politics, and generally fought to improve the lot of the black worker as part of the process of transforming American society. The struggle led by the League resulted in objective improvements in the areas of safety, working conditions, elevation of blacks into positions of authority in local unions, increases in numbers of black foremen, and in the elevation of level of consciousness on the part of the black worker... The League experience has a significance that is much greater than simply a half-decade of struggle in Detroit. An examination of the experience of the League may tell us much about the larger dialectic of race in America."

And in practically all accounts, interviews and reflections on the work, the achievements and the failures of the League of Revolutionary Black Workers that have appeared since the early 1970s, the important role of Michael Hamlin as one of the key organizers and leaders of the organization is emphasized. In their essential history of the League, *Detroit I Do Mind Dying*, Dan Georgakas and Marvin Surkin stressed Hamlin's role as one of the organization's key leaders in the following ways:

- "Hamlin more than any other League leaders, was completely comfortable with all aspects of the League's constituency: its manufacturing base, its white allies, and its community and intellectual initiatives."

- "Hamlin's special talent was to act as a mediator when serious disagreements arose... A soft spoken man of great patience, Hamlin spent hours welding together elements that might otherwise have blown up at each other in fits of anger, frustration and misunderstanding."

- "Hamlin spun a web of alliances and relations for the purpose of creating a good public image for the League and strengthening the links between the various League components... Hamlin also was anxious to see the white radicals in the city form some organization which could act in concert with the League... This resulted in the Motor City Labor Coalition which soon became the Motor City Labor League, a group which at one time or another in its development contained almost all the active indigenous white radicals in the city. The key organizations in putting MCLL together were Ad Hoc and People Against Racism."

By the 1980's, the League of Revolutionary Black Workers and the Black Workers' Congress, its national successor had disappeared but Mike Hamlin continued his work as a teacher at Wayne State University and in the factories of Detroit as the emergency counselor called upon when, for example, a distraught worker with a rifle was about to kill himself and/or others. When Hamlin retired in the early years of the 21st century, hundreds of working men and women gathered at the UAW #600 Hall to celebrate his life and work. And in 2011, Michael Hamlin and Michele Gibbs took the time necessary to reflect on his life, his work and the possibilities of a more just future, reflections which have now been saved and made available in Gibbs' remarkable account, *A Black Revolutionary's Life in Labor.*

ACKNOWLEDGEMENTS

Michael Hamlin

I am indebted to so many people who shaped my life and helped me in doing the work that I felt was necessary in my lifetime. I would say that in the course of my life, literally thousands of people have been receptive to me and have worked alongside me in trying to make life better for poor and working people.

Here I just want to acknowledge some of the people who have been so important to me in my life. First and foremost was my beloved mother who shaped my values and taught me love for people and devotion to family. I want to thank my wife, Joann, who has been my companion - my everything - for more than 40 years. Then there are all of my children, the extended Hamlin family, and my mentor, Garnett Hegeman who have been on this journey with us.

I also want to thank the many persons over the years who have been comrades and friends, making it possible for us to achieve some success in the work that we did. There are innumerable people who have supported me and my family in so many ways. It would be impossible for me to name them all but their contributions have not escaped my memory.

MICHAEL HAMLIN

Among them are dear friends George Colman and his companion, Michele Gibbs, who have struggled along with us since the early 1970's. I also want to specifically acknowledge my comrades in the struggle for justice, John Watson, General Baker, and Ken Cockrel. There are others who have remained faithful friends for the last 40 years: Mike Goldfield, who has been so good to me and my family, Jim Jacobs, Bill Bryce and Bob Mosley who have always been there for me with advice, insight, and counsel.

One thing that I would say is that throughout my life in whatever community I found myself, I never received anything but encouragement and expectations that I would do the right thing and I worked so as not to disappoint those who had faith in me. Whether it was in the cotton growing community in rural Mississippi, the streets of Ecorse, as a worker in Detroit or finally as an open angry and defiant revolutionary, there was always love and support to be found. To all of you, who have been part of my life, thank you so much. I am indebted and grateful.

I would like to thank my wife, Joann, who has supported me throughout this process. Without her help, her expertise and I might add, her persistent badgering, this project would not have achieved a conclusion. I would also like to acknowledge and thank the many people who answered the call to critique our pre-publication draft as well as those who assisted with resource materials supporting the completion of this project: Among them were Aneb Gloria House, Ivy Thomas Riley, Kae Halonen, Bob Mosley, General Baker, Jim Jacobs, Michael Goldfield, Greg Hicks and Rene Lichtman.

Michele Gibbs

I came into the world in 1946 on Chicago's Southside, the only child of radical working class activists Ted and Paula Gibbs. I thank them continually for giving me a world view and an extended community created by their commitment that has proven durable throughout the years. They gave me the foundation for distinguishing who and what were real and the conviction that those like us, with a just cause, would win.

In relation to this book in particular, my thanks go:

To Mike and Joann Hamlin, for staying the course.

To the circle of my sisters in Detroit, whose bonds have strengthened in struggle over 40 years and whose ongoing presence and work together keep me coming back for more... Aneb Gloria House, Edna Ewell, Ivy Thomas Riley, Marion Kramer, Maureen Taylor, Joanne Watson, Elena Herrada, and Lolita Hernandez, June Ridley and Ann Perrault.

To brothers and comrades Charles Simmons, Bob Mosley, and Reg McGhee who, once again, came up with the right thing at the right time. Thank you for still being there.

To George, always in all ways.

And finally, to the people of Detroit, dug in deep, like the river.

*"Each generation must, out of relative obscurity,
Discover its mission, fulfill it, or betray it."*

—FRANTZ FANON

Mike Hamlin, Graduation from Ecorse High 1954

CHAPTER 1

Early Life

"Mississippi God Dam"

—NINA SIMONE

I was born in 1935 in a sharecropper's shack on a plantation in central Mississippi near Canton. I was the eldest
of two children. My father, Edward Hamlin farmed the
land and also made liquor from a still he operated. My
mother Maybelle was an orphan. Her father was the
white plantation owner's son. Her mother had died
young, in her early thirties, so my mother was passed
around to various mean relatives. No one wanted to claim
her. She married my father at 15.

In spite of the fact that my father handled a lot of
money from his still, he squandered it all. Our life was
very difficult. We had to maintain this farm. Fortunately,
my grandmother Magnolia lived nearby and I spent a lot
of time with her. My uncle lived with my grandmother,
and he was a very hardworking man; he was the backbone
of the family. He took after her. She worked constantly. So

did all of my people, except for my father. We worked from the time we could walk.

There is no way one can communicate what work was like in those areas. It was hard; back-breaking; from *can to can't*, as the old folks said. Cotton was still King in Mississippi then. So, when I say "back-breaking work" I'm talking about sunrise to sunset, bent over in a blazing hot field of thorns with a long sack, picking boles from the cotton bushes. Half the proceeds would go to the owner, off the top. The rest would go back to him, too, in the form of paying back what we'd bought on credit from his store.

That was the life. Borrowing would get you through the winter, along with fishing, hunting, and canning. My mother and grandmother knew how to can, and they smoked meat. So, all that was part of keeping people in place while exploiting them. The amount of money that white people realized from the labor of blacks is just incalculable.

As soon as children were old enough, they gave you a small sack, and you would start. Of course, the males, the boys, began to learn gradually the other things that men in those areas had learned and the girls learned from the women. One should not forget that the women, in addition to doing the cooking, the sewing, the gathering of fruits and vegetables and nuts and berries, washing and making clothes, they also worked in the field and birthed and raised their children. Very often, they worked for the plantation owner's wife. This last was the case with my mother.

Everybody knew their place. Blacks understood their place and we also understood that if you got out of place, you could be killed with impunity and without any repercussions. It was just like you would go out and kill a dog today. There would be no arrests, no investigation, no prosecution. You would just be dead.

If someone did get out of line, the lynch mob would be called out. On two occasions, lynch mobs riding with dogs stopped by our place as they were trying to hunt down some folks. They might water their horses, talk to my mother or grandmother to get information (my father was seldom home) and then they would ride on. The interesting thing during the time I was there was the way the community reacted.

In a number of instances when they were hunting black men down, there was almost a telegraph service among us. My folks would get nightly reports of where the hunted person was. They would say, "Well, he made it to so-and-so last night, and he's still running." or "He made it to Chicago." Sometimes you'd hear that they had caught him and that they punched his eyes out, or they castrated him and stuffed his genitals in his mouth, shot him, set him on fire, poured boiling water on him and so forth; whatever ugliness they could imagine. But people were watching. They knew every step of the way when a person was on the run and who did what to him if he was caught.

So, I lived in the country on the plantation until I was nine. I don't remember going to school except for about two years with my sister, in one room with everyone together. Then, my mother, my sister Eddie Mae and I moved to the town of Canton because my father had gotten run out of the state.

What happened was that he was making whiskey. And when you make whiskey, you had to pay off the sheriff to keep him from raiding you. So, my father's still was raided by the I.R.S. They called them "the Revenuers". They didn't catch him but he couldn't make whiskey anymore. That meant he didn't have any money. But the sheriff told him that he had to keep on paying protection, even though he knew he couldn't and there wasn't no protection anyway. So, one day the sheriff told him, "I'll be there tonight and you better have the money." So my father fled to Kansas City where he had some relatives and we moved into town to stay with my aunt.

We had a culture in the South of sharing scarcity. The women were the backbone of this. In ways that would become more apparent to me in later life, my mother, my aunt, my grandmother and the neighborhood women I grew up with shaped me. They were damn near saints. They were always giving. My mother was only 15 years older than I was and I saw her, year in and year out, always deferring, self-effacing, always taking less than she needed. She did that for us and others in the community too.

My father, by contrast, was a very violent and reckless person. One time, my father attacked my mother with a knife and I got between them. She ducked around behind me until she could break for the door. He chased her down the hill in the dark and caught her and almost cut her arm off. Fortunately, a neighbor was coming by and saw them and stopped my father from killing her.

My father was extreme, but he certainly wasn't atypical. My grandmother tells the story of how her husband, my grandfather, had abandoned her with two teen-agers and a baby. They were sharecroppers, too. Each year they borrowed money from the plantation owner to get through the winter and spring. One harvest time, in the early 1900's, my grandfather took the cotton to market as usual. Then he sold the wagon, the mule and equipment and took off for Chicago leaving the family with no money to get them through the coming season. He did not return until about 30 years later. When he did reappear at her front door, demanding something to eat, she grabbed her shotgun. As she pointed it in his direction, I pushed the barrel up so she wouldn't hit him. I was nine years old. He didn't come back.

For many men of his generation, individual escape seemed the only road possible. As for any notion of the future, you really didn't have one. You never went more than twenty miles away from where you were; you had no idea what life was like anywhere else. There were myths and rumors about what was going on in places like Chicago, but it all seemed unreal. Most of the men where we were worked hard, drank hard, played hard, and acted the fool on week-ends. They'd get drunk, gamble, shoot off their guns, fight and sometimes kill each other. They would try to seduce each others' wives. It was just a complete letting loose on week-ends, but that was the extent of it. It was a horrifying world, in retrospect.

It's important to remember that after the Civil War, there was a need to re-establish the plantation system in a way that was productive and enforceable. So, you had to establish a hierarchy: blacks at the bottom, poor whites next, and so on. Given that blacks were in the majority, it was a system enforced by naked physical terror which treated people like brutes. It's no wonder many started acting that way toward each other. Racism in any form anywhere is degrading and humiliating. But in the South, if you were at all conscious, it was just - what can I say - maybe it seemed better to just go out and get wasted on Saturday nights and forget all about it.

If you really go back and absorb our existence through the Diaspora, Middle Passage, slavery, then sharecropping, that life was akin to the Holocaust. It *is* a Holocaust, but over a long period of time. I mean, we ought to have museums in Mississippi like Auschwitz. There are places of infamy all over Mississippi that we should make into shrines. Instead of big death camps, the South had little pockets of them; but everywhere. There are people today who try to deny this but if you look at it, even now, for black folk, North and South, ghettoization, demonization, daily humiliation, topped off by official incarceration and lynching by any name you please continue to be the order of the day. If those aren't the ingredients of a Holocaust, I don't know what are.

So, when I was ten, my mother went up to Kansas City to join my father and my sister and I were left with our grandmother at the house in Canton. I don't remember much about school there but what I do remember clearly is the job I got working at a grocery store owned by a young white couple. They taught me everything and let me do any work I was capable of. I was very proud of being able to bring home $2.50 a week to help feed my family.

Things were fine for about a year. Then, the couple's 16 year-old nephew developed a big resentment against me. He'd take every opportunity to say nasty things to me. One day, I went into the meat cooler to get some meat and he was in there with a knife. He came at me with the knife raised, but tripped and dropped the knife which fell and stuck him in the foot. I don't know if he was really trying to kill me or just scare me. I do know if he had killed me, nothing would have happened to him. I had a couple of those experiences.

In Kansas City my father continued to lead an irre-sponsible life and got into an altercation with a man in a nightclub. He pulled out a gun and shot the man in the knee. So, he was on the run again to keep from going to jail. He went to Detroit, found work in construction, and sent for my mother, my grandmother, my sister, and me. That was 1947; I was twelve. We packed up a few clothes and a bag of chicken and cake and took the train to Detroit. We settled in Ecorse, downriver of Detroit, and lived two families in a project apartment. That was the way every-body did. The ones who had already arrived would take in the new ones and help them get established. That was one of the healthy parts of Southern culture we carried with us.

Ecorse was a small town divided by a railroad track that separated blacks from whites. There was a small group of one-story projects where we lived. These were built during World War II to provide housing for blacks coming north to work in the factories, namely Ford Motor Company, Great Lakes Steel and others. Because there were significant numbers of folk from Mississippi there, it was easy to get connected to a support network.

We arrived in September so that I went right into school. They put me in the fifth grade and my sister, two years behind me. My first day in school, an incident occurred that had a powerful effect on me. The teacher said that I had done something and I replied, "I didn't aim to do it." All my classmates laughed, thinking that this was a funny way to talk. My reaction to that was to keep quiet and listen. I began to study the grammar book that we had so I wouldn't make these kinds of mistakes.

I wanted to learn whatever I was given the opportunity to learn. In sixth grade, I went to junior high school which was part of the high school. I worked hard and got good grades and developed a lasting friendship with Garnett Hegeman. He was at the top of his class, academically and we hung out together all the time. Now, nobody in my home had ever been past fourth grade (some of them said eighth grade to get a job, but it was really fourth).

Garnett's father, a black man, had graduated from Colgate in 1923. He had a degree in mechanical engineering. His first job was as principal of a black school in North Carolina. But, when Henry Ford began to pay $5.00 a day, he left North Carolina, came to Detroit, took a job in the foundry at Ford Motor Company and worked as a laborer for the next 43 years. He also got a mortician's license so he could work at that part-time. He was a wonderful man: brilliant, educated, sophisticated and urbane. But in the 1920's, he had to be a full-time factory worker to raise his family.

The junior high and high school were integrated, probably close to 50-50. We interacted with the whites there but when school let out, they went across the tracks to their side of town and we stayed on ours. As I progressed, I became known for my academic achievements. Garnett's example inspired me. In the spelling bees, I would usually come in second or third to his first. He also taught me all kinds of sports: basketball, football, and tennis. By the time I was in 10th grade, I was good enough in basketball to play on the school team. At the time, I wasn't thinking about football, but we would play on the sandlots and in the street.

One day, the football coach saw how far I could throw a football and spoke to me about playing on the team. So, I agreed and when I went out, he said that because of my height, he wanted me to be quarterback because I could see over the linemen. The person I replaced was a white fellow who seemed to take it in good stride. It worked out and I became a leader of the football team and the star basketball player. I like to think that I handled it with humility because I always had a fear that I wouldn't measure up.

I also became a favorite of some of the toughest teachers because of my work and my sense of humor. During my time in high school, from 1951 – 1954, we developed good relationships across racial lines. In an incident that was quite telling, I led a group of the five top white female students into the principal's office to protest an incompetent Physics teacher who wasn't teaching us anything. I also was able to organize my friends to try to set standards in the school in regard to bullying. We kept the peace.

All this time, I was also working after school. First in a grocery store and as I got older, I switched to a liquor store. My income helped the household budget, as my father continued his irresponsible ways. My motivation always was to do things that would make my mother's life better. I would do anything to make her happy to compensate for the pain and sadness that she had to experience. Most of my friends at that time were going into the plants at Great Lakes Steel or Ford Motor Company. My father told me that he wanted me not to go to college, but to work full-time at the liquor store. I did what I had always done with his advice and I ignored it.

Garnett was going to the University of Michigan to study medicine. He had been planning this for years. As valedictorian of our class, he had a full scholarship which paid all of his expenses. I decided that I would go along with him. So, I applied and was accepted. My high school basketball coach had got me a job rehabilitating one of the elementary schools in Ecorse, so I saved enough money to get me through the first year.

In 1954, U. of M. was a spectacular school of 33,000 students with large dorms and great architecture in a monumental style. At the time I enrolled, I was told that there were 300 blacks in the school. Although most of my friends were freshmen and we were pretty close, this was the first time I was introduced to social classes, especially among blacks.

Nearly all the black students there were middle-class. They were the children of doctors, lawyers, teachers, and other professionals. Only a few were from factory worker families. My thoughts at the time were on the plight of my people, blacks that I left in the South and the people in my neighborhood in Ecorse who were subject to frequent lay-offs and continual hard times.

My problem with the other students was that they were all clear in their upward aspirations. They called it "makin' it", meaning that they intended to be successful economically and their ticket to that was a U. of M. degree. This was also the prevailing ideal in the black community as a whole. I only subscribed to this to a limited degree. Their road was already laid out for them. I still had to find mine.

My biggest problem was money. I had saved money to enroll in school but I had no ongoing financial support. I had a couple of jobs working in a white fraternity house in the kitchen, serving lunch. My mother would send me what she could. But after two and a half years, I gave it up. These were the Eisenhower recession years and the only work I could find was in a car wash. This paid barely enough to eat, let alone, save anything to return to school. So, I decided to join the Marines. I went looking for the Marine Corps office and was intercepted on the way by an Army recruiter who conned me into the army.

Entering the army in basic training in Fort Lewis, Washington, I got off to a poor start. From my perspective, the master-sergeant in charge of our platoon seemed to have developed an attitude of hate at first sight. He brow-beat and abused me from the time that I came under his control until the 13 months that I spent with him ended. As a result, I found myself frequently serving K.P, meaning peeling potatoes at 4:00 in the morning twice as much as any other soldier in our unit. He would frequently find fault with the way I laid my equipment and clothing out for inspection, and anything that he could find, he would cite me and assign me to K.P.

I did enjoy great relationships with my comrades, black and white, although the first night we had a racial fight. We were in Fort Lewis, Washington in barracks called Quonset huts. There were twelve of us living together, three blacks and nine whites. Now, President Truman had desegregated the armed services in the late 1940's but this was still a bitter pill for many whites from the South. Two of the blacks and I were in the middle cubical. Next to us on one side, all of the whites gathered just to chat and we could frequently hear the word 'nigger' being thrown around. By the way, we were all placed there because our names began with the letter 'H' as we had been assigned alphabetically: Hamlin, Hawkins and Hightower. And the big white fellow shouting the slurs was named Holland.

So we went over there where the nine were sitting around and told them that we thought we had been hearing the word 'nigger' being used and that had to stop. We are not going to allow that word to be used around the barracks. Holland said "Well then I don't know what I'm going to call you because that's all I've ever known." He was from Louisiana. "Well, we may have to take this outside." He was bigger than all of us. Hawkins replied, "Yeah, man. I'll fight you." Despite the fact that he was hardly 6 ft. tall and only weighed 170 pounds, at least 50 pounds less than Holland.

The fight began and to our surprise Hawkins hit Holland on the jaw with two quick swings. Holland then charged Hawkins and grabbed him around the waist. To our surprise, Hawkins was able to get a head lock on him and rammed his head into the grill of a parked car. Holland emerged all red and bleeding from various places on his head. That ended the fight and we returned to our barracks and lived peacefully for as long as we were together. The irony of this situation was that Hawkins later revealed to us that he had been a boxing sparring partner with Virgil Atkins, the number one challenger for the welter-weight championship of the world.

The unit we were in was an experimental one and we were put through a number of experiences like three winter months in Arctic conditions and three summer months in hot desert terrain to test men, clothing and equipment in extreme conditions. Most people selected were from the Midwest and the South, representing two different cultures. In the second 13 months, I was in

11

Korea on the DMZ (Demilitarized Zone). I excelled there and became a staff sergeant.

My experience in the army was a major factor in shaping my outlook and feelings about the world. In particular, the evil of the U.S. Empire and its history of wars, slavery, intervention in other countries and development of monstrous weapons, and the impact that it had on all the victims of the people of the world, including those of us oppressed in the United States.

In Alaska, the average temperature was 60 degrees below zero. At the beginning of this winter exercise, we marched from Anchorage and began to climb a mountain, mostly on skis. We left at 7:00 in the morning and reached the top at 12 midnight. My MOS (military occupational specialty) was 112, heavy weapons specialist. Our three-man squad was carrying a Browning automatic rifle and an 81 millimeter mortar with ammunition for both while pulling a 250 pound load on a sled which included a tent, equipment and supplies. Two men were pulling and one guiding, each wearing 90 pound backpacks.

We got to the top of the mountain at midnight and my enemy, Sergeant Vargas called out "Hamlin, you've got the first watch", meaning that I had to walk around the area which had five-man tents and patrol. It was pitch black and there were many places where you could fall off a cliff and, there had also been a sighting of a bear in the area and the Army had hired a hunter to track him down. I patrolled my two hours and woke the next guy.

We had been told that on this march if you dropped out, they would not come back for you. On the ship, there were 80 caskets and we were told that they expected 80 deaths during our exercises. This brought me to understand that my life wasn't worth anything.

During our march, several people dropped out and we assumed that they stayed there or went walking down the mountain and froze to death. However, when we got back to camp, we found them comfortably ensconced in the barracks where they had been for the remainder of our three months on maneuver, leisurely looking for things to occupy their time.

After the Alaskan maneuver, we then moved on to three summer months in the hot Yakima Desert near Spokane, Washington. The desert experience was what you might expect. Burning heat in the daytime, cool nights, rattlesnakes and nothing to do but sit there in the foxhole for weeks on end trying to keep cool in the daytime and trying to keep warm at night.

One of the highlights for me was an incident involving one of the persons who dropped out of the march in Alaska. One morning, we were awakened by the screams of this individual in the foxhole, thrashing around in his sleeping bag yelling, "There's a snake in here; there's a snake in here." We got him out of the sleeping bag and it turned out it was a small mouse that had crept into his sleeping bag for warmth. In the end, the desert experience proved to be uneventful.

After that maneuver concluded, we were interviewed by a group of psychologists from Columbia University to see how people of various cultures react to severe environmental conditions and how our equipment performed. Our testing and training was complete at the end of our first year and we were prepared for shipment to various army instillations all over the world. I was sent to Korea. The war had ended but the U.S. set up a large peacekeeping force which continues today.

Another thing about the military experience is that it drives you more and more toward a nihilistic outlook. It involved a lot of drinking and depression. I think most soldiers go through periods where you don't care whether you live or die. Once your life is devalued, you carry out orders no matter what they ask you to do.

Once you have this mindset you certainly don't value the lives of others, namely the Koreans who were treated in barbaric and inhumane, disrespectful ways. Ways that racist Americans at home reserved for colored peoples. Folks from the South had so much practice, of course, they led the way.

The Korean people had been devastated by this senseless imperialist war and were now, by and large, living in squalor in villages and overcrowded slums in the city. I could see that they had to accept this evil in the same way blacks had to accept it in the South. I could add two and two together and get four. This was 1958. The Montgomery Bus Boycott had happened and Emmett Till had been murdered. The consequences of all this for my friends and me was bitter anger and hatred which led us to more separation, carrying a chip on our shoulders, and being ready to die in battle.

Fortunately, most of my work was commanding a squad of Korean soldiers in construction projects. I was popular with most of the Koreans and had their respect because I treated them with respect and humility. The poverty of Korea was beyond anything I could imagine. In the zone where I was stationed, the soldiers in our unit would walk into any villager's home at any time of day or night, looking for women or drugs. The people endured constant insults and sometimes physical abuse. The biggest industry from what I could see was prostitution.

Here we were in Korea in defense of freedom against communism. After this experience, I never believed that any imperialist war could be justified given the evil, barbaric, inhuman nature of the people in the U.S. that support it. Witness Vietnam, witness Panama and Grenada, witness Iraq.

My final months were spent as an instructor in California at Fort Ord where I trained college students in the

Army Reserves who took the six month obligatory service in heavy weapons. I was officially discharged in 1960.

I was very angry when I returned to Detroit. I started to work as a jumper on the delivery trucks at *The Detroit News*. A jumper was the person who assisted the driver in distributing the paper. I jumped off the truck at the newspaper street box, put papers in and collected the money. I was the third black person hired there, outside of the janitors.

Later, when *The Detroit News* bought *The Detroit Times*, I became a truck driver, a Teamster, and a station manager of newspaper boys. This paid much more money but more importantly in the long run, gave me experience with teen-agers which served me well throughout my life as I worked with young people politically, socially and as clients. I kept this job for the next ten years at which time I resigned after calling in sick to lead the occupation of the Episcopal Bishop's office, part of *"The Black Manifesto"* strategy, which was televised on the evening news. By the time I left in 1970, there were still less than 50 blacks employed there out of a workforce of about 900.

The good news was that after a few months of working at the *Detroit News,* I became part of a cohort of young black and white workers on the dock, who spent a lot of time talking and arguing about politics, particularly about civil rights and the war in Vietnam. Among other things, we organized collections of food, supplies, and money for those fighting the Civil Rights battle for voting rights and against discrimination in the South. The leadership that emerged from these activities was Ken Cockrel, John Watson and me.

When I first met Ken, he was a student in Law School at Wayne State University and worked part-time at the *News*. As I began to drive him to school on my way to work, we bonded as friends and comrades. We spent many hours together in my car and on the delivery truck. We talked politics constantly. Ken was an original, a man with heart, superior intellect and courage to a fault. Ken went on to become a brilliant lawyer with enormous success in earth-shaking trials on behalf of the people. He was beloved by the people and he loved them back.

No doubt John Watson was a genius. Like me and Ken, John was consumed with anger at the evil racism of America. I met John from time to time at demonstrations and when he came to work at the *Detroit News*, he joined me and Ken in our daily rant on the dock. John was an avid reader of Marxist literature and very knowledgeable in various Marxist trends. He was intent and driven with great conviction. This level of commitment, I think, is responsible for both his and Ken's early death.

The three of us were also involved in the struggle against police brutality. A black person would be killed in the community either by a merchant or by the police, and the police would plant a knife on the person who was killed. The police would always be absolved by the prosecutor. We would protest.

We would have meetings and people would be very angry. The lawyers in the Wolverine Bar Association, the National Association for the Advancement of Colored People (NAACP) and the Urban League would all be there. We would decide that we were going to have a demonstration, everyone agreed, and then come the next day, no one would show up except the same group of raging radicals: us.

Ultimately, that process led to a conclusion that nothing was going to be done unless we did it, because the NAACP and those other organizations were gradualists. We were also outraged by what was going on in the South; the beatings, the murders. It was one crime after another. We couldn't stand by silently and in our discussions we realized that we needed a clear plan of attack to be successful in changing things and a way to reach people in the community directly.

John Watson had been all over the map with various socialists and nationalists and any group that was militant and talking about revolution. He shared his experiences and his conclusions that many of these groups had wonderful ideas but didn't do anything but talk. He further concluded that the best idea was from Lenin in the pamphlet "*What is to be Done*" which was to use a newspaper as a vehicle to bring people together and build an organization.

So, John and I equipped a newspaper operation with money that we supplied and founded the *Inner City Voice* newspaper in 1967. We were assisted by black nationalists, artists and young people that we previously had contact with. All of these groups included women. From the beginning of our efforts we have worked with women conscious of the need and supportive in our efforts. We took our paper, which called for revolution, and placed it in stores in the black community.

After the publication of two editions, the nationalist part of the group wanted to force me and John to eliminate articles by or about any persons other than blacks. We, of course, had already established that we were Marxists-Leninists and we were publishing articles by Che Guevara and Ho Chi Minh. John got his friend and comrade, General Baker to chase these folks away. It was General who would become our link to inside organizing in the plant.

Detroit is a working class city. At the time, almost all black families had someone working in an auto plant or a related industry. This gave the city a unique working class character. We understood that workers had power at the point of production and they could use it. By 1968, under the leadership of General Baker, a long-time community activist who had been fired from Chrysler's

Dodge Main plant, we began meeting with a group of workers from the plant. This effort would lead to the establishment of The Dodge Revolutionary Union Movement (DRUM), an organization demanding representation for black workers in the plant.

DRUM began based upon conversations between Ron March and General. Ron, who headed the in-plant DRUM election slate, was not a Marxist but rather a trade unionist and somewhat a nationalist. He was motivated by conditions in the plant and corruption in the union. He articulated the worker's concern in a very powerful way. I joined them and we began with a core of black workers and by publishing a newsletter in the plant called "*Speak Out*".

BLACK WORKERS TAKE CONTROL

The leadership abilities of DRUM and the effectiveness of black workers power were demonstrated in two spectacular strikes against Chrysler Motors in Detroit. The first occurred in May of 1968 when black workers walked off the job to protest racial discrimination, safety violations and poor working conditions. The action shut down Chrysler's Dodge Main assembly plant for four days and demonstrated the power of worker's control at the point of production.

After the Dodge Main strike, the spirit of the action spread throughout the area and ultimately across the country, spawning Revolutionary Union Movements better known as RUMs. There was DRUM from Dodge Main, FRUM from Ford Motor, ELRUM from Chrysler Eldon Road and MERUM from Mound Road Engine. In January of 1969, ELRUM led black workers in a strike at Chrysler's Eldon Road Gear and Axle plant for two days.

Needless to say, these actions sent shock waves throughout the auto industry, causing all board rooms to take notice and ultimately action. Dan Georgakas and Marvin Surkin's book *Detroit: I Do Mind Dying* is an excellent resource for details on these actions.

Later that year, after the ELRUM strike, representatives from the spin-off efforts began to contact us for organizational assistance which we supplied. This plus the community organizations and youth groups we were providing leadership to, made it necessary to create an umbrella group, the League of Revolutionary Black Workers. My role as one of the founders was to see that League policies were implemented and to hold it all together with all the personalities and egos.

What distinguished the League was our ability to engage masses of black workers at a time when many people did not know how to approach or mobilize them. The League was very good at building a broad coalition of forces in spite of all the problems and some of the contradictions in our message. We worked across race and class lines.

Some of the best and brightest people in our community were attracted to the League. We had brilliant legal minds and some of the best in-plant organizers this city has ever produced. Our efforts created quite a stir and provoked concern both at Chrysler World Headquarters and at the UAW headquarters, as well as among the police. It was intense. Our overall line was that: *Black workers were the vanguard of the revolutionary struggle.*

We were not driven by abstractions. Our personal situations were desperate. The one sure thing was that we were not going to continue living under the existing conditions any longer. When we said that we were willing to die for the people, we actually meant it. It wasn't rhetoric. I was committed to be, as George Jackson once said, "an ox for the people to ride."

"A union of workers is power. They can, if they so decide, control the economy of a country as large and powerful as the United States simply by calling a general strike."

THE LEAGUE OF REVOLUTIONARY BLACK
WORKERS-1969

Maybelle Norman Hamlin 1919 – 2006

"Stand for something, or die for nothing."

—J. J. JONES

CHAPTER 2

Conversation on
The Condition of our Condition 2011
with Michele Gibbs

Detroit, August, 2011

Note: When I arrived from Oaxaca to interview Mike for these conversations, I found him gravely ill just released from the hospital after kidney failure. We met twice a week for 6 weeks while he was under treatment. His convalescence continued over the course of the next year while we kept in touch editing and further discussing our conversations.

MG: From your accounts of your early life, it is clear that in your first 25 years you experienced directly 300 years of black life in the U.S. from agricultural plantation to industrial plantation, including 'Buffalo Soldier' recruitment during the Korean War. At every stage of the country's development, black labor was pivotal and structurally central. In this context, reflect on the qualitative differences in our community over the last fifty years.

MH: At each phase of the black experience incidents and events occurred that moved the community's consciousness forward··· wars, for example. On my return from Korea there were probably thousands of us who were perplexed, angry, frustrated and looking for a way to purge the bitterness that had accumulated through the years. We were questioning what we could do. The idea of suicide bombing was very popular. One thing we had in common after coming out of the military was an attitude that it didn't matter if we lived or died. By the end of my military service, I was so deeply unhappy with the state of my life and the conditions of my people that striking a blow against the system by a singular spectacular symbolic act was very appealing. I was angry and I was not alone.

In fact, this era was called the *era of the angry black man*. There was even a *"Time"* magazine cover with a brother draped in bandoliers holding a rifle under the headline, *"The Angry Black Man"*. Having gone the full limit in terms of military service to our country, we expected some changes on our return. But just as after the Civil War, World War I and World War II, that didn't happen.

My experience was that the most advanced, i.e., those who had done the most work, were struggling to find a common approach. For a lot of us that was Marxism, many others embraced Black Nationalism. In addition to acting individually, we were searching for more effective methods of engagement. Marx, Lenin, Mao, Nkrumah, Lumumba, Nyerere, Ho Chi Minh, Fidel, Che, CLR James and Frantz Fanon were some of the influences convincing us to organize our people for power.

During the 1960's SNCC (Student Non-violent Coordinating Committee) was primarily active in the South. Its main focus was voting rights and public accommodations.

Jim Forman was the Executive Director of SNCC which introduced the powerful slogan of "Black Power" promoted by Stokely Carmichael and H. Rap Brown, Chairmen of the organization.

These men from SNCC were powerful fighters in the evil and insane murderous Southern part of the country. At great risk and the loss of some lives SNCC was primarily responsible for establishing voting rights, organizing blacks in the South and raising the consciousness of many of their members both black and white. Their work was primarily responsible for the passage of the Voting Rights Act of 1965. You might say, their bravery uplifted blacks everywhere.

After SNCC dissolved in 1966, there was a vacuum and the Black Panthers picked up the banner. At this time the notion of 'picking up the gun' was very attractive to both black men and women in the context of Robert Williams' and Malcolm X's call for self-defense and self-determination. But for me, a feeling of collectivity and being responsible for our people's overall well-being led me away from adventurism.

In our group, we were studying and studying hard. We had research units. It was very important for us to understand all we could about this system and how it operated so we could carry on the fight successfully. And, as you know very well, in that time intellectual ability was at a premium in our community as a whole. In Detroit, we were fortunate to have people like John Watson, Ken Cockrel and you, who were revered. But the pressure was so enormous, it would break you if you didn't have support.

We were trying to build something together and there were many views on the scope, shape, and overall objectives of what that would be. In Detroit, it led us to organize our organic base, black industrial workers who were strategically placed to shut the system down.

MG: If you think about the internal condition of the black community then, apart from individual leaders, what gave you confidence that you could mobilize and shape that general anger into an actual weapon for change?

MH: I learned from Mao something that has stayed with me forever: "A just cause enjoys abundant support." I knew that to be true, particularly among black people. But you had to articulate that cause in a way people could understand and clearly distinguish your position from opportunistic Uncle Toms who were then and are now rampant. You had to chase Tom and his arguments off the stage. Young people appreciated this. We were young, too.

We knew what we felt and could see with our own eyes and we decided to start our own newspaper to be distributed in the plants and schools to spread our views. I am eternally grateful to Peter Werbe for giving John Watson several months of training in newspaper production which allowed us to develop our newspaper. Of course, John and I had distribution experience in our job at the Detroit News.

The key was we had dedicated people, absolutely committed, come 'hell or high water'. We made mistakes; we rectified them. We forgave each other. And we realized we were learning together. We also found that when the situation demanded it, we could produce three or four times more work than others who were not as focused.

The willingness of youth to work with us also gave me confidence that there was real potential for change that would be taken up by the coming generation. We had a lot of high school and college students around who contributed mightily to all aspects of our work, passing out leaflets at plants, participating in all kinds of rallies, doing office work and writing for our newspaper and newsletters. During this period, I was serving as adviser to Gregory Hicks and the Black Student United Front which organized a network that involved all the Detroit Public High Schools that had black students. I assisted them in publishing their newsletter and offered advice on strategy. They held very successful actions that resulted in significant change in Detroit District high school curricula.

Of course, there were also opportunists around that we had to ferret out now and then, saboteurs, provocateurs and so forth, but we held our basic line of organizing black workers and stayed together. We supported the local Panther chapter but thought they were too crazy in their approach. Our people pulled out due to their adventurism. In fact, many times we had to come to their rescue and, literally, bail them out of the tight spots they got into.

MG: I remember how, in 1972, five Panthers with their children successfully hijacked a plane from Detroit and routed it to Algeria, where they were welcomed as political exiles. Eventually (in 1978) the United States tried to extradite four of them from France and, once again, we were called to testify on their behalf. I, personally, was assigned the responsibility of going to Paris to testify regarding the genocidal conditions in Detroit they were forced to escape. They became known as 'The Fleury Four' and were freed.

You've noted that black folk in the U.S. don't have much opportunity to develop normally and that is a fundamental symptom of our oppression: psychologically, emotionally, economically and intellectually. My question is: how important is territory and being grounded in place, not just ideology, as a source of political consciousness?

MH: People must have trust in those that they take risks with and for. That is not easily accomplished. The most classic example I can think of is our experience with James Forman.

I invited Jim to Detroit at the point when Detroit was chosen as the site of the Black Economic Development Conference (BEDC) in 1969. BEDC was the outcome of the Inter-religious Foundation for Community Organization's Conference (IFCO), an arm of the National Council of Churches. The conference was a forum for deciding funding and organizational support for a variety of programs. I emerged as chairman of the organization that came out of the conference.

Forman had left his brief association with the Panthers on the west coast and I encouraged him to become part of what we were doing to organize a black workers' movement in Detroit. It was at the BEDC conference that Forman first introduced the idea of the "*The Black Manifesto*" (see appendix) demanding reparations for the role that white Christian Churches and Jewish Synagogues had played in the exploitation of blacks.

Jim brought some former SNCC people with him but they were not sufficient to control the outcome of the Conference. The League was hoping to start a movement that forced the churches to face their responsibility for their heinous role in enriching the South and themselves on the backs of slavery and Jim Crow evil racist practices in the history of this country. This was a just cause.

Jim had documentation from allies within the churches and denominations which gave an account of hundreds of millions of dollars that individual religious institutions around the country held in endowments including one in Detroit that had a three hundred million dollar endowment and only 200 members. So, John Watson and I joined with Forman and brought along our reluctant comrades from the League which strengthened Forman's hand and ultimately brought us funding although it was through a back door.

Forman's record was good in terms of his work in SNCC and the content of his writings. But as he became involved in work in the city, the underground (i.e. the word on the street) began to see him as a "control or destroy" type of person. At first, I opposed that characterization and it became a source of tension within our group. The problem was that Jim was eager to establish himself and gain control of our cadres and in order to do that he had to go around me. No one was following his directions unless I approved it. This was not something I set up; it was simply a reflection of their distrust.

Let me say here that Jim did do some good things. But he couldn't control the organization and soon set about linking himself with the most unstable elements in order to spread his influence. He would give people money; spend long hours talking to somebody who was a fool, building loyalty that way. Eventually, this drove him to the conclusion that if he could get me out of Detroit, he would be in control. These maneuvers backfired on him but not before serious damage was done. This was in the Black Workers' Congress (BWC), a formation we organized to extend the work of the League to the country at-large.

MG: Yes. When you, Mr. Chairman, presided over the meeting in which the BWC, under Forman's influence, expelled me, Ken Cockrel, Ted Spearman and Greg Hicks, the leader of our youth arm, it was 1972.

MH: That's one interpretation. However, the way I remember that meeting is different. John, Ken, General and I started this effort. We were together and we held it together and led the development of the organization. At this point, we had some disagreements between the four of us. As a result, there were three splits in the organization: the first with General, the second with Ken and the third with Forman.

The first split was with General and the faction of people who were nationalists and loyal to him. General and I had enough love and respect for each other that to me, this was a simple parting of the ways. There was a meeting, however, where Ernie Mkalimoto, a newly arrived intellectual summarized the criticisms of all the people in the League's Cortland office and some of the factory workers, and presented a series of charges against the leadership. We as the core staff of the organization explained our position and each side in the disagreement went our separate ways.

The second instance is the one you are referring to, the one between Ken and me. Before this meeting took place, Ken and I talked and agreed we were going in different directions. At the meeting, things were said by some people on both sides. Basically, Ken and I disagreed about what needed to be done in Detroit in regard to electoral politics. At this stage, the organization had always been opposed. To bridge our differences, I agreed to take a 'hands off' position in Detroit and focus my efforts around the country in building the Black Workers Congress. There was important work going on in Detroit against STRESS and that was taken up by Ken and turned out to be an important victory. John was weary and afraid of the FBI; he simply walked away.

MG: Yes. Detroit was being used as a 'test case' for police entrapment and murder of black male youth through the use of decoys. Here, the operation was called STRESS (Stop the Robberies Enjoy Safe Streets). Later this became institutionalized in all black communities across the country as an official method of State terror.

We took the position that the Detroit organization's priority should be to battle against STRESS for our immediate survival and that Jim's China trip, the organizational resources committed to publishing his book, *Letters From Afar* and his formulistic approach to our daily struggle was just another form of personal opportunism.

We lost that argument in the context of the Black Workers' Congress but won it in the streets when we formed the Labor Defense Coalition, declared a 'State of Emergency' in Detroit which was a significant factor in paving the way for Coleman Young to defeat police commissioner John Nichols and become Detroit's first black mayor.

So when was Forman expelled and for what?

MH: He was expelled about a year later for factionalism and fomenting division in the ranks. Serious damage was done. The point is that he came into town and tried to repeat what he'd done in SNCC, telling people what to do; and it didn't work. He was out of control and impatient and had no roots in the community. In his drive "to show the Panthers something", he felt that he needed to be seen as a leader in our organization by any means necessary. He couldn't understand that you couldn't just come in and start throwing your weight around.

MG: Yes, the level of argument was so personal and so vituperative that it was hard for me to see any positive resolution internally.

MH: It all came to a head when Forman tried to get the organization to send me to Cincinnati. He even had a woman there for me. I didn't say a word but that was the final straw and the fellows kicked him out.

I guess when you think you've reached the heights and feel yourself falling; you'll do anything to maintain your former position of respect. The lesson is that you can't just play with this stuff. You can't just walk into a neighborhood, declare yourself 'the man' and you're here to save folks. That doesn't work. There were some crazy people we had to deal with then; and even now I think one of the things we have not taken seriously enough is the role of mental illness, the traumatic effects of continuously having your life on the line, that our struggle has to absorb.

MG: Well, as you mentioned, it was hard *not* to be crazy, given all the pressures we were trying to balance and withstand. And as for what is today called "post-traumatic stress syndrome", our traumas were continuous.

MH: When I talk about mental illness in the movement, people think I'm talking about Forman. I think that's because in his autobiography the title of the first chapter is "Driven Insane" but that is not what I am talking about. Some of society's most brilliant people are quite seriously ill with bi-polar or schizophrenic disorders. One of the symptoms of these disorders is the need for power, acclaim and control. I see this clearly now after having worked in the behavioral services field. Unfortunately the movement resisted any attempts that I made to discuss this, for obvious reasons.

CHAPTER 3

Black and White, Unite and Fight

MG: In the late 60's and 70's, you and Ken Cockrel were in the forefront of forging principled alliances between progressive whites and blacks. In fact, with "identity politics" cresting in the 70's, Detroit was one of the only urban contexts in which blacks and whites were able to work together and where whites accepted black leadership. Reflect on your experiences as the one delegated in the League and the Black Workers Congress to do this work.

MH: As the threat of independent black organizations developed and grew, their disintegration also accelerated. Reactionary whites, law enforcement and the Uncle Toms in the city attempted to turn the community against us but didn't succeed.

In this period of pause and assessment, we were trying to shore up the organization internally but the few of us who were doing most of the work were exhausted. We were forced to broaden our contacts to avoid isolation. You would get folks to volunteer to do some things on a case-by-case basis but there was no real ongoing commitment or willingness to sacrifice that you could count on. As a result, the burden on us was tremendous.

Chrysler had subpoenas out for General Baker, Chuck Wooten and others in the leadership. One effect was that General had to leave town for a year and a half to live in another city. Ken Cockrel was not doing day-to-day organizational work. That was not his role. John Watson was convinced that provocateurs were fomenting conflicts between the Panthers and the RNA (Republic of New Africa) and it scared him to the extent that he broke off all contact with us. He thought he, personally, was being targeted for execution by the FBI, like Fred Hampton, Mark Clark, and so many others, and he wanted out. He left his wife Edna and their three young children at the same time. That left me to control the day to day operations and Ken to deal with external relations.

At that time, the Cortland Office of the League was our headquarters and under the cover of the organization's name, some nefarious things went on. For instance, whites who knew of us from other countries would come by to learn and help. They were jumped on and chased out. We had instances of rape, the impregnation of a sixteen year old honor student who had joined our youth arm and so forth. So you could imagine the opportunities that gave official law enforcement to come down on us, on top of the internal demoralization this caused. And I couldn't be there all the time to keep order among these elements.

I have never been an extreme nationalist. I always judged people by what they said and did and how they treated you. And I admired greatly the whites in the city who were committed to anti-racism work including Frank Joyce, Jim Jacobs, and Sheila Murphy. Sheila came from a background in the Catholic Workers Movement and had done community organizing in Detroit. Jim came from New York City to the University of Michigan where he became involved in political activity. Frank was from the Detroit area. They were the serious ones among those that I knew.

MG: Yes, Frank, actually, was one of the few former members of the NSM (Northern Student Movement) and SNCC who understood the call in 1966 for white veterans of the Civil Rights Movement in the South to return to their communities to organize progressive whites. This took the form of People Against Racism (PAR). Jim Jacobs, meanwhile, coming out of the period before Students for a Democratic Society (SDS) was involved in adventurist activity, continued his previous thrust of radical community education and moved "teach-ins" from the elite universities down to the community college level with working class white students and undertook the reform of their education.

MH: During all this time the Panthers were stoking confrontations with the police. This was the context in which I worked to cement relations with serious white folks who had already proved themselves in struggle. It was a case of develop or die. Some of these white people initiated projects that were uplifting to me such as the Three for Three Food Coop, the National Industrial Mission and the Detroit Industrial Mission movement which sought to work within industry against racism and people like you, working with them and using your national contacts to strengthen what we were trying to do in Detroit.

MG: Yes, the intersection of activity between those who were in motion against the war in Vietnam, the national steering committee of RESIST which grew out of the Chicago Eight trial and the willingness of black people like Ken, you and me to develop coordinated strategies for work created openings to do things like host the Winter Soldier Hearings in Detroit in 1969 which brought to light the growing militancy among returning Vietnam veterans and engendered the political space for their own organizational efforts. Also, in 1969, support from RESIST and contacts with *Newsreel*, a New York-based production company, made possible the production of the film, *"Finally Got the News"* which heightened the profile of the League internationally.

MH: The film, *"Finally Got the News"* was a highly successful endeavor. At the time, we understood that to organize people in the community, we needed communication tools. Two major goals of the *"Black Manifesto"* were to establish black printing and film operations as an outreach and educational tool in the black community. We had started a newspaper and Black Star Publishing was working on books. We were speaking in the community, writing articles and giving interviews to radical magazines but our audience was small. John Watson was interested in making films that could be widely distributed. We established Black Star Productions.

"Finally Got the News" was conceived by the creative genius of Watson who worked with progressive filmmakers affiliated with *Newsreel* to make the film. Rene Lichtman, Peter Gessner and Stu Bird were our primary contacts among the group who came out to shoot the film. I was an officer of Black Star Productions and the person responsible for the film once it got underway. Still photos from the film can be found in the appendix of this book, *"Finally Got the News Photo Gallery."*

This film is a powerful expression of the plight of black workers who were originally brought to this country as slaves. As industry replaced plantations as the primary source of capital in the U.S, black workers continued in their role as fodder, an army of labor to be picked up and discarded at the whim of employers, always relegated to the lowest paying, hardest, most dangerous jobs in the industry. The film documents the League's organizational attempt to attack the racist and brutal discrimination that pervaded places of employ-ment in the United States at that time.

At the initiative of John Watson, the film was shown in England, Italy, Germany, Sweden, Palestine and some African countries seeking to establish a link between workers across the world. The film is still in frequent use today in university and community educational settings as young people seek to understand the explosion of rage by black workers of the period using a revolutionary approach to change. Make no mistake, our efforts brought about far-reaching change in the workplace and inspired other movements in the fight against discrimination.

During this period of outreach we were trying to build a network of alliances with progressive organiza-tions and endeavors that would throw some weight to deflect reaction against our efforts. Our outreach was a deliberate effort to protect ourselves and a likely part of the reason why we all didn't end up in prison or dead.

This worked to some extent in Detroit because there was a great hunger on the part of many who were radical whites to work with us. The old CPUSA (Communist Party, U.S.A.) slogan "Black and White, Unite and Fight" although eclipsed by the McCarthy repression, was something we in the League adhered to. I think our success rivaled that of any other city.

MG: Could you identify some of the best results of collaboration that emerged from that period?

MH: What happened was we discovered if you make yourself available to people, they will very often meet you halfway. If you were a white radical then, you were searching for principled black people to work with. Oppor-tunists were plentiful; the white left was as splintered as the black. So the only way you could have confidence in the durability of your connection was through daily practice. It was with those thoughts in mind that I called a meeting to unite local white radicals in a single organization which became the Motor City Labor League (MCLL). The persons involved were Sheila Murphy, Frank Joyce, Hamish Sinclair, and Jim Jacobs. We talked and they agreed. There were some diehards in our group who took the position that if I couldn't trust you once, then I'll never trust you again, ever, on anything. But we moved forward without them and formed MCLL. Sheila became the primary organizer. The group was independent but it had our public support, which was critical.

Then something else happened: the Kennedy Administration had developed neighborhood legal services in Detroit to help poor people with legal problems. A number of young lawyers with radical backgrounds and histories with groups like the American Civil Liberties Union (ACLU) and the National Lawyers Guild came to town. They knew about the League.

When they came here, they needed an orientation to the city and they contacted me to provide it. I let them know what we were doing and how they could be helpful on individual worker's cases and how this fit into our larger agenda. Ken, although he was a lawyer, connected with them through the League. That was very important because they began to see themselves not only as occasionally useful to the movement because of their legal skills but as full participants in a total organizational effort for revolutionary change.

During the Chrysler strike, for example, we had a battery of 30 lawyers ready to record fraud, defend us against police attacks, and do anything else that was required to support us. They were seriously committed.

MG: In 1969, at the point when Forman presented *"The Black Manifesto"* as a way for black people to get funding for ongoing movement work, it involved using progressive white church contacts to argue in support of that. In Detroit, it was a logical development based on the historic cooperation between black and white progressives. Could you reflect on the political dynamics this produced?

MH: It gave us institutional allies that could provide cover and dilute action by the police against us because we could marshal a force of blacks and whites together. In fact, when we started the Control, Conflict and Change Book Club, it met in the Methodist Church.

The money from the *Manifesto* gave us the foundation we needed to support our educational work in the Black Star enterprises. We bought a printing press, for example, and could pay staff in our office. At the same time, one of DRUM's demands included support for the International Black Appeal which called on the UAW to: "End its collusion with the United Foundation. Black workers should contribute only to black controlled charities working for the benefit of the Black community, and the $300,000 dollars in Peoples State Bank in Hamtramck should be removed immediately and placed in Black banks." It also demanded "that all monies expended for political campaigns by the UAW be turned over to the Black United Fund for Black controlled and directed political work."

It's interesting the way all the organizations began to dissolve at this time. We know of the efforts of COINTELPRO (a program put into effect by J. Edgar Hoover to destroy the left including the black movement) to inject as much confusion as possible through infiltration. We also know the effect of the calculated flooding of our communities with hard drugs. But there was also the tendency internally, after some successes, to begin to believe in your own invulnerability. Then personal ego takes the place of group betterment

MG: Let's backtrack a minute to late November 1963. We are in the Greater King Solomon Baptist Church and Malcolm is delivering his *"Message to the Grass Roots"*. Although we hadn't met yet, we were both there. For me, it articulated a worldview that I hold to even now. For example, on the eve of the March on Washington, he told us of the deals made and concluded that the only reason to go to D.C. was to take it over. He placed the objectives of the Black Liberation Movement in the United States as necessarily revolutionary and went on to describe what that meant with international examples. And he attacked the psychological identification black people had with America as schizophrenic.

MH: The identification with 'America as the greatest country in the world' for black and white people is a fundamental myth that must be combated. The list never ends with some folk about all the reasons you'd want to stay here. I tell them I'm just about ready to go and get up on out of here 'cause it's getting worse. Those of us, who really know this country, can't stand it. We know that we're living with a fraud and we're suffering from it. We then latch on to any examples of our people winning something, in sports for example, and identify with their triumphs being ours. I do that now, if I see a contest between a black and a white boxer, for example, ain't no question of who I want to win. It's an identification fueled by centuries of unrelenting pain and sorrow.

Malcolm's 1963 *"Ballot or the Bullet"* provided hope that one way or another we would get some satisfaction in the direction of justice. We had lived our lives being abused beyond belief and not being able to strike a lasting blow against this oppression. So Malcolm comes along, big, bad, and brazen, with a revolutionary analysis and tells us it is logical to pick up arms to defend our-selves. Remember that the majority of the black community then condemned him for the stark nature of his challenge to us, the notion that revenge is deeply rooted in our people and justice demands it. If you contemplate the ongoing outrages we live with---seeing people, family members raped, lynched, butchered, you reach a point of seeking refuge in denial. After all, what can you tell yourself if you know the history? You begin to question how we tolerate it, and worse, praise the system responsible for it. I don't live well with that question, Michele. It can be a dangerous subject with me because I know too much about what was done.

MG: One of the aspects of Malcolm's message to the grassroots which meant the most to me was that it signaled the shift from "speaking truth to power" to actually taking power ourselves. In Detroit, through the subsequent decade, one of the issues in the city-wide movement we were building was the controversy over whether electoral politics was a useful strategy alongside of cadre-building and what priority it should have in terms of resource allocation and programmatic profile.

MH: From the beginning, young black men wanted to fight. We were all suffering under the same blanket of police brutality so we could not consider electoral politics as a viable solution. We had but one thing in mind as militants. Ken was out front with his feelings, as I was. He was a master of humiliation where his opponents were concerned and would give no quarter. We convinced ourselves that, short of just getting some ammunition and blowing up these MF's, revolutionary politics and practice would give us a rationale to keep living. That's how we picked up Marxism: it gave us hope that we could struggle collectively and, hopefully, have some successes. Malcolm shocked the enemy to his drawers and we were ready for his message.

MG: It was also the period when in Detroit, black police were organizing independently in the Guardians and
we had some contact with them as an arm capable of
blunting racist police practices in the community. The
STRESS operation led Ken, myself, and others to form
the Labor Defense Coalition and press for taking over the
City of Detroit by any means necessary, including electoral politics. To quote Ken, at the mass rally at the
University of Detroit in 1972:

"When we analyze the operations of STRESS, which
came into existence in January of 1971, we are looking at
a trail of 14 homicides against black male youth in the
past year. None of the cops responsible have been
charged. This is no surprise. But that stops us not at all.
It means nothing to us. We will abolish STRESS and
continue the work begun by a broad coalition which asks
all people who are progressive to stand up and understand that it is not necessary or desirable for a society
organized like this, which excuses outright murder and
daily degradation, to continue to exist. This is simply
step one in our continuing organizational drive to develop
the power to be able to control and run this city our-
selves: militarily and otherwise."

MG: We were mobilizing thousands at the popular
base for direct action in Detroit, action which helped pave
the way for Coleman Young, then a State Representative,
to return from Lansing to run for mayor of Detroit and
win.

MH: The movement took a turn then, away from our
original thrust. Some spectacular things were done which
had an impact but overall, we were far short of our goals.
Thinking about it now, even with all of our problems, I
felt better about our position than I do now. Now we can't
seem to do anything to confront these folks effectively. It
seems they can do whatever they want to and we take it.

If you look at the way the city is deteriorating, the way the politicians like Dave Bing are picked out to run because they can be easily manipulated by monied interests, we should be in motion but we remain silent. It's pitiful.

All of a sudden, in the late 1970's, everybody was running for something, it didn't matter. They got reduced to pawns in the game. After Coleman Young's administration, Ken died and all the blacks who held office here were either caretakers for the establishment or crooks, and the crooks have the upper hand. Ken Cockrel Junior (after his father's death) was an interim caretaker but that didn't last long.

The shift, without much discussion or debate, took place from our side because Ken saw the possibility of wielding more influence that way. He had a love for the spectacular gesture and he knew that he could accomplish dramatic things and he didn't want to accept limits. The organization at this time was also floundering, although we didn't appreciate how badly. There was just conflict everywhere. I couldn't stand trying to mediate those vicious confrontations between people who were theoretically on the same side.

The Motor City Labor League was also undergoing a split at this time. We had gone full bore for several years under all that pressure from the police, from our families, and the churches, to desist. It was burn-out time. There were many personal break-ups too. You have to be ready for the long haul.

I knew that Ken had always planned on running for office. In fact, I was his first campaign manager when he was living in the Jeffries projects in the 1960's and ran for State Representative. He had tremendous magnetism. But the rest of our organization was not going in that direction.

MG: One of the themes that you've highlighted is that even if individuals do have a lifetime commitment, we did not have enough bench depth to structure an internal division of labor that was supportable or for the leadership not to get burned out.

MH: These organizations mirror society and are highly susceptible to bullshit, especially when individual desires for fame and public recognition take the place of the long haul. Then, with increased visibility, individuals not in the leadership start calculating how you can hustle in the name of the organization. This was especially a problem at the organization's entry level.

MG: Have you reflected on whether 'democratic centralism' as an organizational form contributed to the problems people were having? Did it strengthen or weaken the movement at that point?

MH The fact is that the rank and file and also some of the leadership could mouth the words but didn't fully appreciate the meaning of democratic centralism and how it should function. There was never an adequate educational preparation of the rank and file. The random activity became too much to absorb or change. Some elements seemed impervious to correction. In the beginning, every member of our organization was required to be a worker. That was basic. If you didn't work somewhere, you didn't count. Meanwhile, the demands intensified and we had to work with folks who didn't have jobs, weren't interested in getting them, and were only mouthing revolutionary slogans. Macho psychology kicked in and a lot of enemies were made. Work in the plants also suffered. Too much time had to be devoted to cleaning up messes. So, when we were effective, it was often in spite of our membership.

MG: So, by 1973, with the election of Coleman Young as Mayor, there was a shift from complete militancy to effective cooperation.

MH: Exactly. Coleman tried. He tried to take care of people and defend the city. But he was the last one. When such a development occurs, you must pay attention to the alignment of forces. It was not a universal wish to see Coleman Young in the Manoogian Mansion, just as it was not the wish of the power structure to see Obama in the White House. To ignore that, to think that you can move a black into a position like that which is dependent on financial support from people outside of his control and to think that they will go along with his agenda, is nonsense. It is not to understand the fundamental reality of racism in America. What keeps this country going is racism. It is necessary for 'stability.' The white ain' gon' let the black get anything, particularly if it involves power.

One of the things the American working class has yet to face is how racism blocks their progress at every turn. Obama's election has driven them insane and they have allowed reactionaries to grab and hold the initiative. Now, it's not possible to put together his original coalition of forces. The working class has allowed this and been complicit in letting white reaction dictate and manipulate the terms of the discussion. Formal union membership is down from over 30% in the 1960's and 1970's to under 10% now and it will continue to fall as corporations continue to roll back and wipe out all the material and political gains workers made since the first Depression in the 1930's.

MG: So, with a more and more inchoate working class, there is generalized confusion, desperation, and anger without any class-based, work-based, regional or national programmatic thrust to show how their best interests can only be served by getting into progressive motion together.

MH: Are you familiar with the concept of "scapegoat"?

MG: Familiar with it? We are it, repeatedly.

MH: It's the working class that has dropped the ball. The whites have a level of comfort they don't want to lose and they are caught subjectively between envy and jealousy. With jealousy, you love the object you are fighting for. Envy means not only do I want what you've got, but I don't want you to have it; and I will destroy you or it, no matter what, even if I can't get it.

You take one of these whites, and they'll grab you and jump over a cliff just to kill you, no matter that they'll go down, too. There is a program out there for scapegoating and it is naïve to think that simple logic can combat this mentality. It is in their literature now. They tell you straight up who they hate and blame and the race war they are prepared to wage to 'come out on top' and save the country. Blacks don't believe it because it seems too horrible to accept; but it's true. They constantly raise the threat of Al Qaeda exploding a 'dirty bomb' in the U.S.; it is more likely to be a white American racist.

MG: The corporations have already been unleashing a continuous barrage of "dirty bombs" for years. The levels at which those in charge of social policy are killing us is pervasive; from incinerators in communities spewing toxic air, to fracking, mountaintop removal, urban removal with freeways not only cutting off and demolishing our neighborhoods, but also wiping out the memory of what was once there, to the prison/industrial complex. The genocidal pattern is there. We continue to be the ones on whose backs the contradictions of this society rest most sharply.

MH: Right now, they're about to wipe out my sister's whole neighborhood, downriver, on the edge of Ecorse. They have been inhaling fumes from Marathon gas as long as they've lived there, and it's killing them.

MG: Even in the 'Greening of Detroit' movement currently underway here, once people do begin to transform vacant lots into community vegetable gardens, they are discovering that the ground they have just broken is radioactive. Chemically charged.

MH: It's a hell of a thing. A city of farms. Back to the first plantation.

MG: Well, at least back to a small-scale independent subsistence economy. As one black farmer told me, "We ain't planting cotton." I think the thrust of this energy on the ground is part of a global understanding of 'the common' and peoples' current struggles for control of the natural environment and their right, minimally, to be able to feed themselves. For black folk here, it is a return to a politics and practice of self-reliance.

CHAPTER 4

The Positive Channeling of Rage

MH: I left organizational work in the middle of the 1970's as a matter of personal survival. By this time, I was married to Joann Castle and we had a child. The revolutionary period had passed but my passion to make a difference continued to burn. I understood that I would need to find a way in this new period to continue to do work that was consistent with my commitment to serve the working class and humanity in general.

When I met Joann, she was a mother involved in the radical Catholic movement for justice. She came to me with a lawyer friend of hers during the time of *"The Black Manifesto"* with evidence exposing corruption in the Catholic Archdiocese's mishandling of Poverty Program money intended for poor people in the city. Joann and her friend were organizers of Hourglass, an organization demanding the Archdiocese hand over vacant church properties in the city to the black community. She was a member of the Ad-Hoc Action group against police brutality, and the Motor City Labor League. When Jim Forman and his family moved to

Detroit, they lived with Joann and her family. As we became friends, Joann and I conceived the idea of the Control, Conflict and Change Book Club and program. We married in 1975.

It was time to step away, reassess and regroup. We should at least be able to help people one at a time. Go back to school, get degrees, and re-engage from another point of entry. This worked for many of us who had been in the movement. Our idea was that everyone needed to discover some work that was useful on a daily basis. Also, I needed a source of income that was stable and adequate to support my family. My primary criterion was that it would be something that would give me the satisfaction that I was helping workers and the poor.

My interest in social work came about based upon my relationship to three social workers I met in the movement. I greatly admired Clyde Giles, a professor of Social Work at the University of Buffalo who moved to Detroit to join in the work of the BWC; Don Bagley was head of a community organization sponsored by the Interfaith Council of Churches on the northeast side of Detroit; John Williams was in the League and then the BWC. Each of these men had outlooks that focused on community service. With their support, I felt that I could succeed in the field and accomplish my goals of helping but I would need to get a degree.

I approached Clyde Giles about enrolling in Wayne State University Master's Program in Social Work. By this time, Clyde was on the faculty of Wayne State. Even though I hadn't completed my undergraduate degree, my years before the Army at University of Michigan and my community experience counted. I had gathered a great deal of knowledge in my experiences over the last 10 years and I had good contacts who I knew would support me. They knew me and some had worked with us.

My application to Wayne State was rejected the first time by an Uncle Tom, black capitalist social worker, who owned six McDonalds and was in charge of the minority opportunity grant program in The School of Social Work. So, Clyde began to organize the faculty to support my admission, which succeeded the following year. I entered the program in the fall of 1976. My focus was community organizing. My intent was to take a low profile and meet my academic requirements.

I made lasting friendships at the university with students and professors including Marianne Mahaffey, a long-time Councilwoman and President of the Detroit City Council. Three students, Jerry Clark, Maria Guadiana and Joseph Gorham, all political activists were in my classes and were very close throughout our school experience. Our left-leaning professors treated us like colleagues. I was the only one in my group of friends who had a small child. Since my wife worked, I sometimes took our young son who was three or four years old to class with me or on campus where my friends and I studied and hung-out to discuss politics.

My intent in the school was to do my studying, hustle money any way I could and maintain my family. But because of my newspaper experience I got talked into becoming the editor of the Social Work student newsletter. Then a situation developed. One of my dear friends, Maria Guadiana, came to me and told me about her first day in her group work class in our second semester.

In the class, the instructor who was an elderly man, said to all the students that he wanted the black students to know he understood they couldn't do college-level work but if they just showed up for class, he would give them a 'B' which was necessary to stay in graduate school. He also said that the Hispanics were the same and Native Americans, we don't expect anything from you.

I, of course, didn't believe this so I checked with other friends and they verified what Maria had told me. I was enraged and I knew that I had to blow my cover so I came out with a two-fisted article covering the front page of the student newsletter, blasting this individual who had been a beloved old professor driven to this madness allegedly because of his daughter's involvement with a black pimp in Boston. I was approached by several professors who were friends of mine asking me to give him a break but they knew this was an outrage. After that, everybody knew who I was but I was still able to graduate. Except for this incident, my experience in the school was wonderful.

In my program field placement, I got the opportunity to work with black small businessmen in the community, helping them get organized to better serve their clientele. In my role as a community organizer, I was able to help them become more politically active as well as more profitable in the commercial strips they occupied on the near Westside of Detroit. But this was not the only transition I was making.

As my family responsibilities grew, I became more disciplined and more responsible. It was a complete transformation. I never had kids before and I was learning what it meant to be a parent. The birth of my first and only natural child gave my life a kind of purpose that I never had before. My wife had children before we married so I became a step-father as well.

During the period when my wife was working full time as well as going to school full time, I also took on responsibilities in the home so that she could focus on developing a career in health care. Joann left early in the morning for a 7:00 am shift at a nearby hospital. I would drop the children at three different schools. On evenings when she was in class, I learned to get dinner on the table, oversee homework and encourage the kids who would open up to me, to problem-solve issues in their lives. I tried to encourage all the children to think about their futures. As a new father, this wasn't easy but it was rewarding.

I had always loved working with young people but before I had children, I did not understand the joy they could bring to your life. Although it was sometimes awkward being a step-dad and I'm sure for the children to be step-children, in the end it seemed to work out just fine.

I had always dedicated my life to the idea that I wanted to make life better for those around me. This was true in my early life and it carried with me into my new family life. I wanted our kids to be self-sufficient, able and accomplished. I often pushed them; in some cases indirectly through their mother. In my view and to my satisfaction, they have all become good and successful human beings with a conscience and concern for others.

My career in social work has been everything I hoped it would be. As I gained experience, I found that I was able to influence practice in a way to better serve clients. I listened to people and they listened to me. As I moved to more responsible positions, I gained experience in my field.

I had managed many enterprises in the League, the Black Workers Congress and the Black Economic Development Conference which had given me management experience. I was interested in social work administration as I wanted to set policy. My first job after I graduated was administrative assistant to the Executive Director of the largest senior network in the city, Adult Service Centers. My boss, Mickey Allardyce, was a long-time leader in Gerontology and Mental Health. I learned a lot from her. I left the agency a few years later, when she told me that she could not promote me to a job that I was entitled to because a long-time employee would never accept me as her supervisor.

Then I moved on and for a couple of years I worked with Donald Roberts where I managed a drug treatment program for heroin addicts, many of them workers. Don was an early supporter of the League who had started and continued to direct a large social service network, Neighborhood Services Organization.

The thing that drove me hardest during these years was the pain of knowing that my clients were in a never ending situation and the realization that this was systemic. First I worked with the elderly, then addicts. But there weren't resources to produce any useful results. Finally, I got the opportunity to garner some power to intervene positively.

I moved into the Employee Assistance field when an ex-classmate's husband who often hung-out with us on campus, decided to open a behavioral services business. He recruited me on the basis that he needed a black person who could work with industrial black workers in an Employee Assistance Program (EAP) to serve troubled employees. This was a joint program supported by the auto companies and the union. It was ironic that my salary was now being paid jointly by management and the UAW. This reflected in many ways the success of our efforts in the League to demand respect for workers.

So, I was hired by Occupational Health Centers to act as their Senior Clinician in the metropolitan Detroit area. Our biggest contract was with Ford Motor Company but we also contracted with many other small companies throughout the state. We were diagnostic and referral therapists (CDR) and our diagnosis had to stand up against insurance companies and providers including psychiatrists and psychologists. In my first year, I served over 800 clients. We worked with couples, children and anyone else referred by the UAW or the company. Policies were inclusive rather than exclusive. This gave me broad contact with the masses of workers, an ideal situation for a revolutionary who wishes to serve the people.

The insurance companies were screwing workers out of their benefits and here I come, championing the workers. And I was successful, not only with advocacy for rank and file workers, but also for many of the children of UAW members and their families who had succumbed to various forms of addiction and needed rehabilitation programs, not necessarily in the city. I was the one who made special arrangements for treatment with insurance companies and company human resource people. This enabled me to get things done for troubled employees and their families of both union members and managers. Many jobs were saved and families re-united.

The tragedy of racial division within the working class has never been taken on with any kind of significant effort or results. Management and select union leadership and rank and file racists continue to exploit this condition. This exploitation leads to frequent conflict between black and white workers and sometimes results in violent incidents.

For example, one day Oliver French, a black electrician who was also a committeeman, shot and killed his plant chairman and bargaining committeeman and wounded two other union officials. I was called in the next day. The place was in chaos. Since I had experience chairing meetings and I was seen as being fair in my judgments, I once again, became a trusted spokesman for workers' grievances in this situation. Also, I had been a sergeant in the Army. It all helped to restore order. So, I had a commanding voice and I knew these people. They were just like me. I knew their fear and also that they had no other choice but to show up to work, 'cause come Friday, your family would need that paycheck.

The French incident is typical of workplace violence. Workers face a multitude of social and economic problems at work and in their home lives. These can stem from financial problems, marital problems, and resentment or personality problems on the job. There can be competition for job advancements, affairs in the workplace, unfair labor practices, race and gender issues; the list is endless. Management and unions must be proactive. They must recognize the possibility or probability that this kind of thing can happen.

Ideally, there should be a policy of zero tolerance for violence or threats of violence in the workplace. The company and the unions have joint responsibility to engage the workers and educate them on the possibility of incidents so that they know where to turn at the first sign of a problem. We should couple a zero tolerance policy with a resource base such as an Employee Assistance Program with qualified counselors, psychiatrists and medical doctors that can be summoned at a moment's notice. I recall an incident when I was called because a worker at Ford Motor World Headquarters was in a closet-sized office with a gun. We responded immediately and an incident was avoided.

Sometimes people get fired or suspended or just plain crack under pressure. Through the program, they can be put on sick leave from their job by a psychiatrist while they receive treatment. In this way, problems can be addressed to keep the environment safe, help troubled workers receive treatment and then regain their positions in the workplace.

For instance, the Oliver French incident was a narrow conflict over a split in the union caucus. All persons injured or dead in the conflict were friends who were involved in a bitter power struggle and a fight for control. Those who were close to the situation may have been able to help avoid this carnage if they had understood the importance of seeking help for an aggrieved worker.

After this incident, I was often called on to deal with the tragedy of workplace violence. The broadness of my background gave me skills that were useful in these types of situations. I continued to do this work throughout my years as an EAP. I was used at places of employment throughout Lower Michigan to stabilize workplaces in the aftermath of violent outbreaks and empowered to deal with these traumatic incidents through the support of the UAW and Ford Motor Company.

The 1990s was a decade of mergers and takeovers in the insurance industry. As a result of a merger, I found myself with a new employer, Value Options. This company had broad responsibility for managing workers' insurance in a humane way. In fact, Value Options was the second largest mental health managed care organization in the country. One of the things I discovered very early was that clinical jargon was used to bamboozle clients, union and company representatives and enabled the insurance company to deny service, save money and lose the client. We put an end to that.

In this position, I had social work interns from Wayne State University, University of Detroit/Mercy and Eastern Michigan University placed with me. The placements were based upon an understanding that many of these young students would be entering into this growing field from upper-middle class families and might never have had contact with an industrial worker, especially a black worker.

I was able to get things done for my clients and I was consistently rewarded for my advocacy by the workers, the union, the company, my employer and some providers. The work that I did and the relationships that I established with the union representatives in the plant went very well. As a result the union reps demanded that my boss appoint me as the first black company vice-president.

Also, with the support of the UAW, I forced the service providers to give us a list of minority clinicians on their staff so that requests by clients for a therapist that they could identify with could be honored. While I was there, the organization enjoyed great success and has maintained these contracts until today, in spite of lavish lobbying by competitors to take away their business.

At this point in my life, I experienced an acute incident of heart failure. After I was discharged from the hospital, I was told by my doctor that my condition was severe and that I would not be able to work again. This was heartbreaking. I retired in 1999, but my reputation had been established and many people, whom I worked with like Jim McNeil, then President of UAW Local 600 and Bob King, Vice-President of UAW-Ford Department, were in a position to validate the contributions I had made. I was completely overwhelmed when a retirement dinner was organized in my honor by Value Options, Local 600 and Ford-UAW International. I would never have imagined that. But it showed how workers are: If you take care of them, they'll take care of you. They definitely took care of me.

CHAPTER 5

What is Your Analysis?

MH: If young people today want to learn from our experience in dealing with an organization and leading, they need to understand what it means to answer the question, "What is your analysis?" John Watson used to start every conversation with that question. And, if you would ask him, he would give it to you. So we got into the habit of sharing our understanding of each situation as it unfolded. People now, if you walk out here and ask that, what do you think they'll say?

MG: Diabetic?

MH: Probably. We tried to give people a structure to develop a thorough political and economic analysis to guide them in determining who are their enemies and who are their friends, and where they should focus their main efforts. That's what is missing now. The hope is that young people will be like we were and get a full grasp of the stark reality of the black condition. That they will understand the situation of blacks in this country does not make sense, is getting worse, and ask where are we now, collectively as a people, in spite of Obama? If I had come of age in the beginning of the 21st century as a black man in dire circumstances and saw the desperate needs of black people, I would be forced to speak out and resist. And as you know, every now and then, if you work with young people, poets, for example, you can hear some profound expressions of understanding.

MG: I'm glad you said that because in former years a range of activities that were dismissed by some people as *narrow cultural nationalism* in fact produced an outpouring of visual, written, and musical statements that penetrated the popular mind a lot more deeply and in a radical way than some of the social policies we proposed, the long meetings we had to get to the point where we felt we could go out and represent the best interests of the community.

Right now, I think that in the absence of both individual and organizational leadership, people are drawn even more to cultural expressions because you don't need a plan; all you need is a stage. You don't need an organization; a wall will do. And you've left your signature on the landscape of our neighborhoods as a spiritual presence of resistance. I give thanks for it, but also understand that it is a symptom of the absence of other channels for effective political engagement.

MH: I can see the flurry of artistic activity. It feels as though we're once more at the beginning of something. And since the death rate among politically conscious black artists is not as high as among black radical political leaders, there is an opportunity for more intergenerational mentoring and continuity. Amiri Baraka is a case in point. And you're right; it penetrates.

Even so, you look at the situation and can also despair at the prevalence, for example, of hip-hop themes of sexual exploitation and promiscuity, and the acquisition of money and what it can buy; the overall thug culture glamorized. All of this is extremely corrosive.

MG: As time goes on, I think rap is superseding hip-hop in very telling ways. A lot of the young brothers are taking the standard set by Grand Master Flash in the early 1980's and extending it. Also, the musicality as well as the message is coming back. On the positive side, witness K'NAAN from Somalia, but bred in the Bronx, and John Legend's new CD, "*WAKE UP!* " And in the realm of performance poetry, Sunni Patterson, out of New Orleans, is in a class by herself. I think even the average young person, plugged into their iPod is clear that the same monied franchises that pump negative images into our community on a multiplicity of levels are also responsible for promoting the skewed emphasis in the music.

MH: It is not that the youth aren't open to ideas. I still teach part-time in Wayne State's Africana Studies Program and you should see the response of my students in classes dealing with racism. They are hungry for an analysis that makes sense.

We became Marxists in the 1970's because we discovered it was a tool for revolutionary analysis and leadership. Marxism offered guidelines to assess our current situation and determine what the tasks were. From this, we would develop a strategy which directed our path.

Young people can develop this capacity by studying the works of Marx, Lenin, Mao, Ho Chi Minh and other revolutionaries learning how to identify the main contradictions in society. On the one hand you will find the contradiction between the working class and the capitalists; on the other hand, the contradiction between blacks and a ruling class that needs their cheap labor to succeed.

Also, integrated into studies of revolutionary history has to be the particular history of the U.S. working class and the use of race which has kept the working class divided throughout our history, thereby keeping capitalists in power. Sometimes it seems that we go from day to day, just living, doing whatever to make ends meet; we don't have the energy to get a perspective.

MG: One of the things you noted before is the extraordinary energy produced when you have an analysis, a group to sharpen it, and you are in motion for the community. And, of course, one of the strategies of pacification is to make you so tired, and bombard you so constantly with doublespeak that you can't extricate yourself sufficiently to think straight. All you want to do is sleep, by any means necessary.

MH: The only thing keeping me from actively organizing anything now is that I know I couldn't maintain the level of energy required. You can't start something and think it will take on a life of its own. You must be there to sustain it. So, when I talk to young people, I emphasize this. Know that it requires a lot of work, primarily from *you.* I go on to tell them that social science is a science, not just a compilation of empirical statistics. The way they have been taught doesn't allow them to analyze the social situation that confronts them. If you have an analysis that allows you to understand the contradictions you face on a daily basis, it makes you less dependent and less vulnerable. That is the missing ingredient that needs to be reintroduced.

MG: True. Just as ridiculing the prevailing stupidity, although easy and popular, even cathartic, isn't sufficient. Just keep laughing...as they taze you to death, arrested for moving while being black.

CHAPTER 6

Detroit

MH: A full analysis of Detroit requires an understanding of black people. We are a complicated people who have remained largely inarticulate because we have been prevented at every turn from getting any traction in the direction of justice.

We came from the South with powerful yearnings, which made us absorb everything we encountered. Even more important than numbers was our position in the working class. We had come to work and were organized. And we were an extended community who were forced to protect our families collectively. We had the hardest, most dangerous, and dirtiest jobs; but we had hope. We thought we could make it on the strength of our own attributes. I know I did. Eventually, we learned about second-class citizenship, but for the first time, we had money. And others resented it, often with disastrous consequences. Houses were burned, crosses put on lawns, young blacks were murdered by police and civilians --- but we stayed.

Of course, the first thing Southern blacks would do after they accumulated a bit of money was to buy a car which they helped produce, some new clothes, and go back home for a visit to demonstrate their success in their new life to friends and family, with great visibility. That was obviously not palatable to whites who had no such finery to display. This rekindled resentment against us because it showed we could leave and achieve.

So, as our afffluence increased, we wanted to move up. And for every individual attempt made, white resistance increased, particularly in the area of housing. The message was: "We'll make room for you… but be sure you stay in your place."

Then, individuals were selected to act as intermediaries between the community and various institutions. Often blacks who were active in establishment politics operated to keep the majority of us in our places. The police were, by and large, white ethnics who wanted to be cowboys and they operated as a terror force. You could only stay out of trouble by not complaining and keeping a low profile. This was the environment and it was not an easy thing to conform to it.

On the other side, Detroit in the 1930's and 1940's was home to a large and powerful progressive labor movement which included black activists like Horace Sheffield, Buddy Battle and Coleman Young, who cut their teeth in the Congress of Industrial Organizations, the CIO. Later on we met James Boggs and progressives Marty Glaberman and Dave Herreshoff. These were forces that greeted us, treated us decently, and extended their hands. We appreciated this. And we built on it.

The seeds of rebellion and resistance are deep in this city, generation after generation. From being the last stop on the Underground Railroad, to Ossian Sweet, from independent black caucuses to revolutionary politics in the auto industry and beyond, each era has added something new to the legacy that has not dissipated.

Now, a movement may be warranted and even justified at many points. But in order for it to be activated, it
needs people to take the first step --- to sacrifice themselves. In 1968, we had to be crazy enough with rage to
shut down Dodge Main at Chrysler. If the police were
called, it could mean that black workers would be shot
down like dogs. But the wrong was so bad we couldn't
endure it. So we were willing to take the steps necessary
to lead our people into struggle. The same was true in
SNCC and the Freedom Riders earlier, as you know well,
Michele. It took young people to give their lives. We were
ready to do that too.

Detroit in the 1960's was home to a large, organized
industrial proletariat. The auto companies were going
full steam in terms of the number of cars being produced
and the number being produced by workers per hour on
the assembly line. Signs on the freeways kept car production numbers scrolling past like a pulse of the city.

It was characteristic of the new left to declare that
the working class had no revolutionary potential and that
our future lay in the hands of students and youth. Some
of the older leftists held the same view that youth on the
streets held the power for change. The most vocal propo-
nent of the potential of black workers at the point of
production as the revolutionary vanguard was John
Watson who worked tirelessly at spreading this doctrine.

When we emerged with the Inner City Voice proclaiming that black workers were the vanguard with
DRUM validating it in action, the League grew rapidly.
The word was out. Young white radicals and some blacks
moved here to participate in what was happening in
Detroit. We advised the whites to go into the plants and
organize in their communities. A lot of them maintained
a limited relationship with a few of us. We incorporated
the blacks into the League structure.

The reason nothing is happening now is that the radical vanguard isn't ready. Just like the Middle East today, it takes a critical mass to be so fed up that they, themselves, take leadership despite the consequences. Nothing else matters. You need some satisfaction.

Today, young blacks here are focused on how other blacks are oppressing them, stealing, killing them, raping children, without considering the larger picture. The self-loathing that results is amazing. Not to mention the gutting of public education which previously acted as a space where young people's consciousness had a chance to expand.

MG: Yes, now the colonial status of our people is being brutally enforced.

MH: This is the resurfacing of the original right-wing agenda, Social Darwinism. Let the powerless perish, and make sure that they do. The historic role of academia in justifying this ideology through Eugenics and other bogus social constructions has done and continues to do terrible damage.

In the absence of a revolutionary movement in Detroit, opportunists have seized the time in most government and city institutions as well as segments in the trade unions. But we still have hope. This city has an important progressive history, still has a large working class, a large black population and many people with a radical political consciousness. Detroit is a sleeping giant. Oh, to be young again.

CHAPTER 7

Critical Mass

MG: On the subject of 'critical mass' and the importance of population density, Bob Mosley, a brother from Pennsylvania who came into our orbit through being a conscientious objector during the Vietnam War, remembers the impact made on him seeing Dodge Main for the first time:

"People often forget that at its height, Dodge Main employed 70,000 people. I had never seen such a concentration of potential power. The size of the working class, it's density in Detroit was completely different. And you guys were organizing them? Against management and union racism, too? This was serious and it led me to work in that plant as an organizer for the next five years, until 1978."

MG: By the late 1980's, though, we get to the point when a lot of the identifiable male leaders died. Heart attacks, strokes, cancer, years of unrelenting pressure, old age and the ravages of AIDS in the artistic community took a heavy toll. We entered a narrow careerist period for the aspirations of the next generation of black youth, with community engagement seen as a 'distraction.'

Meanwhile, corporate auto executives, absorbing the real threat to the status quo that our activity had posed, continued to decentralize, automate, and internationalize their operations. In the language of Marxism, they "exported the contradictions." So, in the 1990's, you had to start from before scratch to develop a new population with critical consciousness. Also, aggressive policies of urban removal, rising street crime, and red-lining practices forced an internal redistribution of our people, either into the suburbs (like Southfield), or chasing employment in some other state. So, there was a geographic diffusion of energy in the community as well, even before the economic crash we are experiencing now.

They stabilized the industry, and marginalized us. Now, the strategy involves moving whites back into the city they gutted and recruiting professionals internationally from countries like India and Pakistan to develop 'new technologies.' They call it "resettlement." What effect does that have on the people who have been here all along?

MH: Yeah. We now have the option of being farmers, prisoners, or mercenaries. We have been here before. Plus, what happens to dying civilizations and dying cities is that people degenerate into barbarism. People are starving out here. And the right-wing agenda is to roll back and cut off all recourse for relief – food, medical care, education, social security – programs that the working poor, unions, and progressives have battled to put into place since the Depression of the 1930's and World War II. If you add in domestic surveillance and warrantless wiretapping, it is clear that we are living in a police state. But, it's part of our collective denial to refuse to recognize how dire the situation really is.

Another problem right now is that when you start trying to build something, those who show up are either sectarians or opportunistic politicians. Both elements are only there to 'recruit a dupe' to their existing program. When we got started, and not only us, but the Panthers, the RNA, (Republic of New Africa), Malcolm and the OAAU (Organization of Afro-American Unity) we knew that you could not just get out there and run your mouth, regardless of consequences. Now, the disrupters are succeeding. Plus, the 'sound bite' has replaced analysis and volume drowns out reason; and the most vehement arguers are also the most ignorant.

So, I always tell folks who have grown up arguing with teachers, parents, with bosses, with cops, with lawyers, and who have been resistant to any control, that saying "no" is not enough. This is true on the white side as well as the black. The Tea Party is one manifestation of the effectiveness of ignorance in this period.

MG: What are some of your reflections on the state of the labor movement today?

MH: In the UAW today opportunism is rampant and getting worse. It began with Emil Mazey who chose Uncle Toms for positions our militancy opened up.

MG: Yes, Bob Mosley also recalls how "At Dodge Main the 'action group' included Joe Davis, a total sell-out and opportunist who was a forerunner of today's revisionists. He tried to assume the mantle in language, but without action. In fact, his job was to see that nothing happened. He became head of the Civil Rights Division."

MH: Also, the caucus structure is locked into the national and people get positions based on what political support they can command and the favors they can dispense, not the ideas they have or their opposition to the status quo. To rise, you must make deals. Even Bob King, President of the UAW, after a long history at Local 600 of principled advocacy of workers' rights, is restricted by the short-sighted old guard. Plus, he only has one term. There are many honest trade unionists, but they are not organized as an independent force.

MG: Now, with union-busting rampant, and a two-tier wage structure at the entry level in auto, the overall economic crisis is used as a pretext to divide the base and further individuate people's relationship to production. Workers are just 'hanging on', going along to get along.

MH: The economic situation combined with right-wing Republican reaction against President Obama, is rolling over all independent voices and there is very little the union can gain. In fact, they're trying to break the unions entirely. These blows are demoralizing, but not necessarily fatal. AFSME (American Federation of Municipal Employees), the Machinists Union, the UAW and the Teachers Union are still among the most progressive voices, but they're under serious assault. This is real class struggle, but the enemy has most of the weapons on their side and control of the political apparatus and most of the news media.

The interesting thing about it is that Obama and the Democrats don't know how to fight. Here, the Democrats and Obama saved the auto industry in spite of Republican efforts to kill it. Come the 2010 election, who do you think some of these white UAW workers voted for? Republicans. Now they're losing pensions, healthcare, and jobs. The President can unveil his jobs plan, and it might even be a good one; but it ain't goin' nowhere.

The question is whether we are witnessing the real collapse of global capitalism and what we plan to do? What aspirations are real and what is an appropriate response in this situation?

MG: Since we know very well that we can't make a revolution in one city or one state alone, although you can make some steps in the direction of rationality, and we've identified the quickening pace of the immiseration of the multitudes worldwide, what are the transformative sources of energy you would point young people toward now?

MH: The Mideast is where the vanguard is today. As an imperial power, Europe has long lost the capacity to lead; its time has passed. Even the US, with its wars against the guerrillas in Iraq, Afghanistan and Pakistan, has gotten stretched too thin and does not have the objective capacity to lead unilaterally. The question is not so much whether the forces of domination will prevail as whether they will collapse. The other question is whether there is another place for capitalism to go?

MG: You mean, can it regain any kind of equilibrium and continue to dominate?

MH: Yes, what are their plans that are real?

MG: Let's say that international capitalism cannot self-correct and the damage already done to the biosphere, etc., is so severe and irreversible that the question of what *we* plan to do takes on a different dimension than ever before. Capitalism has, in fact, become its own gravedigger and time is running out.

MH: You are absolutely right. There is no guarantee that anyone will come out of it. You said the other day that it's either socialism or barbarism. And the insanity of these capitalists in pursuit of money knows no bounds. Look at the Japanese situation: earthquake and nuclear meltdown and their government denying how serious it is. After that, even the Germans halted their nuclear program in response to popular demands. Meanwhile the U.S. under Obama, a liberal, continues to build new nuclear plants and keeps old ones in service that are springing leaks all over the place. The warnings are there and they are consistently ignored. This is what is so incredible.

In order to maintain control, U.S. capitalism has purposely created a general population which is ignorant, self- defeating, and self-deluded. They have made being *dumb* the objective. For instance, they argue that global warming doesn't exist, against all scientific evidence. What kind of world are they living in? Pure fantasy. This is extremely dangerous.

Another thing I learned in the 1960's was that those in control will fight tooth and nail, no holds barred, to crush any challenge to their rule. We know what they are capable of in terms of brainwashing and misleading. For instance, we must not forget the Gulf of Tonkin incident when President Lyndon Johnson fabricated an attack by Vietnamese boats on a U.S. ship as an excuse to escalate the war in Vietnam. There was also the claim of weapons of mass destruction in Iraq and other times when the U.S. has fabricated a crisis in order to initiate military action. Also, let us not forget that the U.S. is the only nation in history to use a nuclear weapon on a civilian population in the Japanese cities of Hiroshima and Nagasaki.

MG: Witness Cuba, Grenada, Panama, Iran and Afghanistan, just to name a few.

MH: The current situation in Libya is more complicated. But the United States objectives remain the same. Conditions are ripe in a number of spots, but subjectively, in the U.S. folks aren't ready.

When we emerged on the scene in the 1960's, the revolutionary movement was confined to a few enclaves, not just in the U.S. but internationally: there was Vietnam, Algeria, and Cuba. We had connections there as well as with formations like the IRA (Irish Republican Army). Today, the movement in resistance to capitalism and imperialism is once again global and opportunities for mutual support are tremendous. The changes in technology have helped this development and the youth have been critical in realizing the political possibilities of electronics.

MG: Yes. For example, WIKILEAKS (an on-line, not-for-profit website that publishes leaked documents exposing government and corporate misconduct) has been very effective as a whistleblower on the criminal actions of the U.S. government in Iraq and Afghanistan. And without blogs and social networking, we would not even have access to on the ground reporting from uprisings in the Middle East. It's a different world. We thought we were doing well to move from mimeo to offset printing to spread the news.

When we speak of youth now, it's also important to remember the changing demographics of age. In Mexico, for example, where I live, half the population is under the age of 25. This is a growing international reality.

MH: The main questions for us in the 1960's were: where was the revolutionary potential located? What was the role of the working class in that process? And, did the working class have any revolutionary potential? That was apart from the black struggle. We asked: "Where are the people who are disciplined, informed, and willing to take the most risks?" We came from an industrial base and became those vanguard voices in our generation. And the base identified with us. The only reason we weren't smashed entirely was because of our base. And rhetoric alone won't do. You have to back it up.

MG: Since you said the word 'base', I want to add here that the role of black women in building and sustaining a base of support, both organizationally and in the community, was pivotal in Detroit. Whether it was Helen Jones running the printing press or Edna Ewell Watson being a militant activist in the Hospital Workers' Union Local #1199, or Marion Kramer (Baker) being office staff as well as being rooted as a conscious mother and wife of a revolutionary leader in the neighborhoods of Highland Park with police on the wild, or the ranks of young sisters ready to hand out leaflets at plant gates, our consciousness and commitment matched that of the brothers, though from a different point of entry.

To quote from *Finally Got the News:*

"Black women are in struggle due to sheer bread and butter needs. We are relegated, by and large, to low-paying, high-turnover jobs. Over 40% of us are service workers. We are the maids and janitorial workers who clean the houses, the floors and walls in the office buildings and hospitals after white women secretaries and white collar professionals leave to go home."

"Labor Dept. studies report that an increasing number of black women will soon be hired into manufacturing in hopes that due to our desperate need for better employment, we will be less militant in pressing for our rights than black men. But we understand better than anyone else how much work goes into every pound of bacon, every slice of bread, and we know what it means to be laid off. We, more than anyone else in the workforce, know what it means to be looking, always looking, for work. We have the highest unemployment rates and the lowest wage scales. In spite of our needs, we continue to be the last hired and the first fired."

These conditions, combined with the police assault on young teenage brothers, were the driving forces that made us all the more militant. But that was in 1969.

MH: It is hard to do justice to the contributions made by the women of the League. In the beginning, women were the backbone of the office work, passed out leaflets and performed supportive tasks. As time passed, we began to see them as revolutionary comrades capable of anything that the men could do. At that time, society in general was just beginning to be challenged by a new generation's militant demands for women's liberation. However in the black community and the black working class of Detroit, sexism and male chauvinism were rampant.

Despite this reality, our women became involved knowing that they had something important to contribute to the cause. We were under enormous pressure from parents, spouses, friends and family members, demanding that we stop our activities, stop wearing our hair natural and stop putting ourselves at risk in the streets. For women, it was even worse. Nevertheless, we had many brave, educated, strong and beautiful sisters who were always with us. An example was John Watson's wife, Edna, a stalwart who raised their kids and contributed what she could, including financial resources to help launch *Black Star Productions.*

At the beginning with the *Inner City Voice*, women were limited to part-time efforts in order to minimize the opposition of the people who cared about them. I recognized that the women of the *Voice* were revolutionary comrades and in fact, like all of us were being transformed as we fought. I tried to practice and hold other comrades to a moral standard. As DRUM developed locally and the League was born, the women grew in numbers and contributed to moving the organization forward.

The most notable among our female comrades in the League were Helen Jones, Marion Kramer, Cassandra Smith, Yvette Baker, and Mabel Turner. Helen had skill as a printer. She was instrumental in the successful publishing that we did. Helen worked as hard as anyone in our organization. Lynn Edwards from New York was the first woman on the Central Staff of the Black Workers Congress. I won't try to mention all the women who joined the BWC. Many of them were from cities around the country. All of them took part at great cost and great sacrifice. Possibly my deepest regret is that we could not curb, much less transform, the doggish behavior and chauvinist attitudes of many of the men.

MG: Well, as one of the only black women of that period besides Marion Kramer who maintained a national movement profile throughout the 1970's from a base in Detroit, I just want to add this. Precisely when the male-led organizations were disintegrating, the women's movement was gaining ground in the black community. Many of us who were forced apart by organizational splits maintained our personal connections. We met in our own consciousness raising groups and brought up children together.

Ideologically, we attacked both the class and race bias of the dominant bourgeois feminist movement. We created our own texts and became our own authorities. We published. Politically, we organized the fight against Patrick Moynihan's formulations on the "*Black Matriarchy*" and the punitive social workfare legislation and forced sterilization it justified.

We connected with Third World women's groups throughout the hemisphere and formed our own international alliances. We formed organizations like the Third World Women's Health Alliance and spearheaded the Pay for Housework movement as well as NWRO (National Welfare Rights Organization). Similarly, the Detroit perspective was heard in 1976 at the founding Conference of Socialist Feminism through the keynote speech I was invited to present. Networking replaced tight organizational forms and we were known to each other through our work.

The relationships built then continue to this day. In many ways, the decade of the 1970's was the Black Women's time when our voices were finally raised, en masse, uncensored, and we were able to fundamentally change the national discourse on the scope and record of women's consciousness and activity for at least 50% of the population. Anyway, all of that merits its own discussion.

MH: As the League reintroduced the class question into the progressive movement of the 1960's and advanced black women began to move independently, class and race were similarly foregrounded in the women's movement through their insistence. No matter how ripe objective conditions are, the subjective factor, that is, the consciousness of the people is critical. It is also important to have people who can lead by personal example.

MG: For many of us, the lines of struggle internationally as well as domestically, were drawn in 1955 at the Bandung Conference in Indonesia, the same year that Emmett Till got lynched in Mississippi. At Bandung, an analysis emerged which correctly pitted the Global South against the Global North. It extended W.E.B. Dubois' pronouncement of 1909 that "the problem of the 20th Century is the problem of the color line" and oriented us toward the geopolitical considerations that continue to be primary today.

Now, if you ask people about the Non-Aligned Movement, they'll probably refer you to a chiropractic surgeon. So, my point is that in addition to being willing to take personal risks, leaders must be able to articulate what historical traditions, events, and experiences their decisions and priorities flow from.

CHAPTER 8

"To be or not to be
is not the question"

—T-SHIRT SLOGAN WORN BY BLACK YOUTH IN DETROIT.

MG: A lot of the project-based leadership I came in contact with this past year during the U.S. Social Forum in Detroit, attended by 16,000 community organizers, surfaced from unexpected places in different forms. Black Men United in Omaha, Nebraska, for example, working with brothers coming out of prison and returned vets from Iraq, focuses on psychological counseling as well as skills training and political education. Their question is, "How can we repair the severe damage that has already been done?

The Latin American and Caribbean Solidarity Movements have taken on new trenchancy due to the presence of significant numbers of people from those countries living in the U.S. The Palestinian support movement now includes Christians, Jews, and Arabs who are clear that Israel is the aggressor in that conflict.

As a 'movement building' exercise united by basic principles, the Social Forum has facilitated multi-lateral connections for future work together. At this stage, for this generation, I think it constituted an appropriate preparation for the shape of things to come. The very dispersed nature of this aggregation of forces is also an expression of their awareness that we are living in a police state and the less 'formal' our profile is, the harder it is to control our activity.

MH: The understanding that the police state is a reality is a powerful organizing tool, in itself. For young brothers now, jobs and the police state are a good point of entry for action. But what do you think, Michele, of black women's current consciousness?

MG: The family as a conceptual unit in the black community has outstripped any other form of identification as something you're willing to fight and die for. We're strapped culturally with a fundamentally patriarchal model, despite the variations of extended family structures that continue to sustain us. The average black women's consciousness is caught in a cycle of men and children, in other words, the biological reproductive cycle.

Its most negative face, promoted incessantly on daytime talk shows like Jerry Springer and yes, Oprah too, rely on airing 57 varieties of domestic dysfunctionality and go no further in terms of our daily lives. Then, they leap to the stars and individual triumphs over various addictions (not including our collective addiction to television): men, food, chemicals of various descriptions, physical implants and other artificial means to increase sexual allure, etc. Ghetto to Hall of Fame with nothing in between is what is being projected. The message is we can all metamorphose from Precious into Jennifer Hudson. It isn't that progressive black women's voices don't exist. They are silenced. Ask yourself why, for example, in 25 years of programming, Oprah Winfrey has never had a program on Marion Wright Edelman or Maxine Waters, just to name two.

We talked about this before in the context of differentiating between leadership and celebrity. Most people, who are so bombarded by the media that they are vulnerable to pre-packaged everything, go for the 'brightest lights'. For me, this is the most difficult subjective factor to combat among women, particularly when those touted as "Black Public Intellectuals" offer a critique that is so weak, it's no wonder that Queen Latifah is more attractive. Nor is it a surprise that the hard-core bitterness of rap and hip-hop is preferred. It's more honest.

With the exception of the Freedom School Movement, which continues thanks often to the children of SNCC veterans, and which seeks to intervene where public schools fall short and charter schools are too expensive, the organized challenges to the prevailing bullshit are scarcely there. Just like you were saying, Mike, in relation to Obama and the Democrats, it seems as though this generation of black thinkers don't know how to fight and don't care to learn.

At the same time, the overall level of formal education for black women has increased exponentially since the 1960's. In Oaxaca, Mexico, where I live, I come into contact with a continual stream of sisters between the ages of 18 and 30. This cross-section of sisters, studies, travels whenever possible, comes to Oaxaca, often from the historically black colleges like Spellman to learn Spanish and to acquaint themselves with the African presence in Mexico. Their world-view is not bounded by the urban tenement or suburban enclave they grew up in. Most of them, although eager to explore the world are ready to understand in a fundamental way, for example, that the struggles and condition of the African world are central in determining the survival of the whole planet, only have a very specific set of skills they feel comfortable contributing to 'good works'. The question of leadership definitely does not come up. If they can be of use in a small way in the context of the structures that are already set up, they are satisfied.

MH: That is all that's being asked of them.

MG: That's right.

MH: Given the opportunity, however, our experience shows that they will be forced into the front lines as they meet frustration at every step.

MG: Whether they want to take on that burden, or not. The older generation has already 'passed the baton,' so to speak. We'll see who takes it up.

MH: It's more than a notion. What I have learned is this:

You have to love and be for the people in an obvious way. You must learn what work is required and with whom. This involves learning about others outside your immediate community. You have to have the capacity to attract all types of people and impress them with the immediacy of the cause, making your cause, theirs. You accept what people are willing to give and provide a context for that to be helpful. You must be willing to engage in the 'culture of argument' fearlessly. In the black community, you've got to 'barbershop.' You also must have a palpable force to draw on to give your opinions weight. One voice alone, no matter how righteous, is not enough.

The intensity of this commitment will transform you. I was just a guy from the country, but the situation forced me to grow. We were driven to develop. And finally, you must be willing to sacrifice your individual advancement in service to the whole, speak the truth, show the way forward, and be prepared to deal with the consequences.

MG: How do you view the current anti-corporate popular upsurge epitomized by "We Are the 99%; Occupy Wall Street" movement?

MH: Of course, it is wonderful to see these young people and some seasoned voices too, come out and demonstrate in this spectacular and spontaneous way. Such action cannot be denied by the ruling class and the movement will have to be pacified. However, I view it in the way that the Bolsheviks would. There need to be three components in a revolutionary situation. First, the people cannot live in the same way and, the ruling class cannot govern in the same way. What the situation today lacks is the third component, a revolutionary organization rooted in the masses with the working class to lead it. Thus far, it has been emphasized that this movement has no one set of leaders and its agenda is being developed on the spot. Nevertheless, they do have a general statement of principles and may have the fortitude to force some reforms, as has been the case in times like these in the U.S. before.

I would also say that this situation is unlike the Middle Eastern *Arab Spring*, where you had organized armed groups with help from various outside nations and groups in Egypt and Libya. That will not happen here. Ultimately there will be a reform that will calm the situation. Although I would caution that non-violence begets violence and this has happened already with 700 people being arrested on the Brooklyn Bridge and with people filmed as they are beaten by police without provocation. Expect more of that to come and intensify.

This may be the beginning of this generation's long struggle for an end to this monstrous empire. Now, after two months of street actions nationwide, it is clear that a large number of people have come to understand the bankruptcy of America. It couldn't be clearer than it is today that the nature of capitalism is to maximize profits on the backs of the workers. Marx predicted the ultimate impoverishment of the working class, no matter how developed capitalist productive relations became. At last, the people understand what is being done to them by the corporate class. As they lose their jobs, their homes, their health care and watch the devastation of the public education system all accompanied by unparalleled gains in wealth by the corporate class, they realize that they have been screwed.

The 99% Movement has responded by coming together in a sustained and enormously powerful effort that has already made some gains in changing public discourse and affecting small concessions from corporate powers. The movement is diverse, tremendously energetic, creative, and it shows promise. While it is very early, we see this development as a broad social movement with global implications. While built on the backs of earlier efforts for change, this movement is different in that it does not have a unitary or clearly defined leadership. We can only hope that this is the first step in imagining a new society, and perhaps new approaches to change that reflect the world in which people find themselves.

MG: Yes. Now that the first hurdle has been cleared and the movement has successfully resisted definition as a fringe element phenomenon, several programmatic directions have already arisen, including disinvestment initiatives in favor of community co-ops, banks, resisting fracking and the Alaskan pipeline as well as the general demand for jobs, a moratorium on evictions, and the Constitutional right to claim and occupy public spaces.

The next test will be what percentage of the 99% will be satisfied with the "piece of the existing pie" they will be offered, and what percentage don't like pie in the first place and want to create a whole new menu and recipes to go with it. For example, I can see calls for a Constitutional

Convention coming out of this process. The unfolding conditions will create appropriate leaders and is already beginning to do so.

On a personal level, as we remember well, those on the ground in this movement are being transformed on a daily basis by their interactions with each other as well as the powers that be. My hope is that we are finally witnessing the shift in consciousness that puts an end to the myth of American Exceptionalism and galvanizes a new generation that identifies objectively and subjectively with the majority of the world's people and faces squarely the contradictions inherent in their own situation in 'the belly of the beast.'

CHAPTER 9

Some Accomplishments of the League of Revolutionary Black Workers

MH: I believe that it is important to summarize the accomplishments of the League. Among the things we contributed were:

1   We focused the struggle for change on the working class.

2   We forced the UAW and unions across the country to change their racist policies and practices by seeing that black workers had a chance to hold office in the union consistent with their numbers in the labor force.

3   We forced Chrysler management to elevate blacks to supervision and management positions. Other large industrial organizations saw the handwriting on the wall and followed suit.

4   We educated and mobilized black workers and their allies in a broad fight for justice.

5   We raised the class-consciousness of young black people in numerous cities and got them involved in the black movement.

6   We broke through and dismissed the shackles that McCarthyism had put on leftists and progressives by openly proclaiming that we were Marxist-Leninists and that we were ready to fight anybody over that right.

7   We organized and raised the consciousness of several groups of white revolutionaries, progressives and liberals.

8   We developed a publishing operation that produced newspapers, newsletters, pamphlets, and two books.

9   We organized a well-attended book club that met monthly to discuss radical and revolutionary books. Lecturers at the discussions were often authors of the books.

10   We developed a movie production unit that produced the film, "*Finally Got the News*" that is still in circulation 40 years later, including use in many black studies, sociology and history classes at the university level.

11   The successes that we had brought about pre-emptive change in workplaces across the country.

CHAPTER 10

Chronologies of Political Involvement

Michael Hamlin

My affiliations over the years reflect the developments in my political consciousness. A partial listing of these affiliations is:

1954-57	NAACP, University of Michigan
1960	CORE, Detroit
1965-67	SNCC, Detroit
1967	Co-founder *Inner City Voice* newspaper
1968	Co-founder & Chairman of DRUM
1968	General Manager, *The South End* student newspaper
1969	Co-founder League of Revolutionary Black Workers

1969	Executive Board and Chairman of Black Economic Development Conference (Black Manifesto)
1970	Co-founder Control, Conflict & Change Book Club
1970	Co-founder The Alliance
1969-72	Co-founder & Director, Black Star Publishing Corporation
1970-73	Chairman, Black Workers Congress
1973-74	Steering Committee African Liberation Support Committee

Michele Gibbs

Organizing committee, member of:

1969	Winter Soldier hearings regarding war in Vietnam
1970	League Revolutionary Black Workers, Black Star Productions
1971	Black Workers Congress
1972	Labor Defense Coalition
1972	State of Emergency Committee to Abolish STRESS
1973	Campaigns to reform jury selection process and to elect Justin Ravitz and Sam Gardner to Recorders' Court
1976	Madeline Fletcher Defense Team (trial in Flint)

1976	Association for the Improvement of Minority Employment (A.I.M.E) class action against Detroit Edison
1978	Campaign to elect Ken Cockrel to Detroit Common Council
1978	Executive Committee of DARE: Detroit Alliance for a Rational Economy
1986-88	Editor: *City Arts Quarterly*, Detroit Council for the Arts.

CHAPTER 11

Coda In Two Voices

JUST WAIT

You see, I remember
when the Detroit Movement riffed.

We didn't only write our politics;
we sang them to the world,
acted them out,
harmonized as one,
and cut a record for all time.

Even when we marched, we danced:
out from the plants
with manifestos
calling for Black Power
in a black town's
Revolutionary Union Movement hour
onto the rooftops and into the streets
closing down the assembly line
"Cause we don't mind workin'
But we do mind dyin.'"

and "we finally got the news
how our dues were being used."

As the blind led the blind ·
not over a bluff –
but to a land Stevie Wonder full
where we had
"just enough for the city."
and we defined "What's Goin' On"
spelled out R.E.S.P.E.C.T.
for more than one generation.

Yeah, those were the days
when what was said
burned in the heads of
hundreds of thousands
and led us to do
whatever we had to
in pursuit of life,
liberty, and justice, too
'Cause "ain't no stoppin' us now."
and we trained our feet
to step to a beat
that shook the foundations of power.

Oh, yeah.
We had more than one hour of triumph
on the stage –

*beat back the police in the form of STRESS
*defeated a racist police commissioner
to elect Coleman A. Young
Detroit's first black mayor
*reformed the jury selection system
*enforced residency requirements for cops

A BLACK REVOLUTIONARY'S LIFE IN LABOR

*freed the New Bethel Panthers, Hayward Brown,
Madeline Fletcher, and James Johnson
*ran for office independently and won
*won a class action AIME'd at Detroit Edison
*DARE'd to call for economic redistribution.

That was the '70's
And we weren't playin'.

But all that was smashed.
Replaced by stadiums and casinos
though you can hear
the songs on CD
and maybe even
up the next alley.

That is our hope:
that the songs never die
as with the movement and memory
their lyrics imply.

Yeah, nowadays
Motown's energy
lays in the wings
preparing –
for a gig, a call, a cause,
a moment worth interrupting
our daily practicing
in woodshed's underground
solid brick houses,
or public places
reclaimed for a hot minute
before sunset
in the too brief summer.

MICHAEL HAMLIN

We still be here,
but dug in deep like the river
implacably blue,
dense hues mirroring our faces,

the current, our voices,
willows, our tendency to bend
just so low before springing up
to seize the next fresh breeze
and blow with it.

Yeah.
We timing our entrance
for the up-beat.
And don't worry.

We ain't never been late.
Just wait.

—MICHELE GIBBS

UNTITLED

Cities have died, have burned,
Yet phoenix-like returned
To soar up livelier, lovelier than before.
Detroit has felt the fire,
Yet each time left the pyre
As if the flames had power to restore.

First, burn away the myths
Of what it was, and is –
A lovely tree-laned town of peace and trade,
Hatred has festered here,
And bigotry and feat
Filled streets with strife and
Raised the barricade.

Wealth of a city lies
Not in its factories,
Its marts and towers crowding to the sky,
But in its people, who
Possess grace to imbue
Their lives with beauty, wisdom, charity, and truth.

You have those, too long hid,
Who built the pyramids,
Who searched the skies and mapped the planet's range,
Who sang the songs of grief
That made the whole world weep,
Whose Douglass, Malcolm, Martin
Rang in change;

The Indian, with his soul
Attuned to Nature's role;
The sons and daughters of Cervantes' smile,

MICHAEL HAMLIN

Pan Tudeusz's children, too
Entrust their fate to you;
Souls forged by Homer's, Dante's,
Shakespeare's, Goethe's, Yeat's style.

Together we will build
A city that will yield
To all their hopes and dreams
So long deferred.
New faces will appear
Too long neglected here;
New minds, new means will build
A brave new world.

—DUDLEY RANDALL

Detroit's Poet Laureate

CHAPTER 12

Detroit Artwork by Michele Gibbs

APPENDICES

APPENDIX 1

PHOTO GALLERY

FAMILY AND FRIENDS

Mike and Joann with son, Alex at 15, 1991.

Mike and Joann visit Michele in Oaxaca, Mexico, 1995.

General Baker speaks at Mike's Retirement Dinner, 1999.

Bob Mosley speaks at Mike's Retirement Dinner, 1999.

Mike and Garnett Hegeman reunite at Alex's wedding, 2005.

Mike, his Mom and sister, Eddie Mae, May, 2006.

Mike and son, Alex on Father's Day, 2010.

Mike and Joann celebrate their 35th Wedding Anniversary, 2010.

"FINALLY GOT THE NEWS"

"We finally got the news ..."

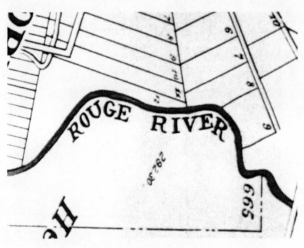

Detroit, home of auto plants and the UAW.

Black workers had concentrated power in the plant.

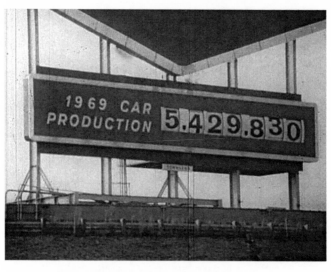

A car production sign on Detroit freeway.

The UAW Flying Squadron allowed us to pass.

Dodge Main tried to get rid of General Baker.

John Watson: "Safety conditions don't even exist."

UAW means "U Ain't White".

Ken Cockrel: Blacks objectively are
the vanguard of struggle.

Our first step was to publish a newspaper:
The Inner-City Voice.

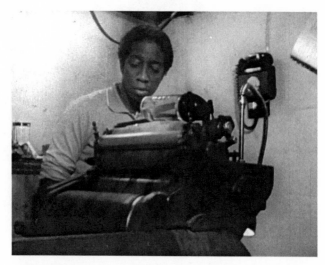

Helen Jones was our lead printer at Black Star Productions.

Workers & students pass leaflets prior to walk-out.

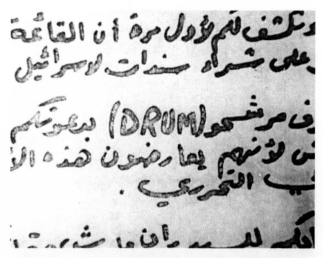

We sought the support of Arabic workers to join DRUM.

Discontent spreads to other plants across U.S.

Ron March: DRUM's hotly contested election.

The League pickets the UAW convention at Cobo Hall.

A black student congress formed.

Women played a critical role in our success.

APPENDIX 2

DOCUMENTS

SPEAK OUT, IN-PLANT NEWSLETTER

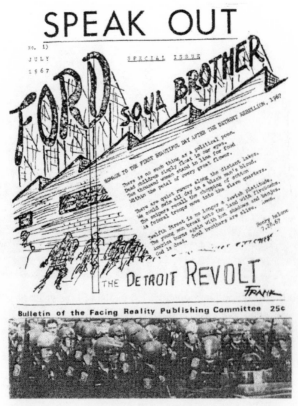

Speak Out, In-Plant Newsletter, July 1967 edition
Michele Gibbs Collection.

DRUM PROGRAM MATERIALS

Dodge Revolutionary Union Movement (Drum) 1968.
Election Poster Materials Courtesy Of General Baker.

Photo of Election Slate poster: Dodge Main Chrysler Plant 1968

MICHAEL HAMLIN

DRUM

Programatic

Demands:

1. Halt U.A.W. racism. 50% representation for black workers on the international executive board. Fire Reuther and elect a Black president and one Black vice president, 50% of all international staff members should be black. Open skilled trades and apprentices to any black worker who applies. Recognition of DRUM and its affiliates as the official spokesman for Black workers on the local and national level with the power to negotiate Black demands on the company and union and the power to call officially sanctioned strikes.

2. We demand that the grievance procedure be completely revised so that grievances are settled immediately on the job by the workers in the plant involved. The grievance procedure is used to prevent workers from using their strike power to fight abuses from management. Since the procedure completely ties the hands of workers and basically serves company interests it should be scraped and replaced by a completely new system, eliminating the company's rights on safety. The U.A.W. must fight for the right of workers to control changes in production standards in the plant.

   The company will not have the right to indiscriminately place workers on new jobs, or harder jobs. Currently workers can challenge the decisions of the company after they have been implemented. We demand that the workers have the right to challenge any decision affecting them before those decisions are executed.

3. Elimination of all safety and health hazards in the auto industry. This means cleaning the air in the foundry and redesigning dangerous machinery and cut back in production on hazardous jobs, and that safety rules be adhered to. The U.A.W. must establish safety committees in every plant. These committees will have the power to shut off unsafe machines, and, if necessary, to close down entire plants because of conditions which are unhealthy or unsafe for the worker.

4. The union must fight vigirously against speed up and increases in production standards. The companies should double the size of their work force to meet the present workload. There were 650,000 production workers in auto in 1947 producing 4.5 million vehicles. In 1966, 650,000 workers produced nearly 10 million vehicles loaded with accessories and options. We are

working two and three times as hard for the same real income. With today's technology production standards can easily be cut to reasonable humane lines.

5. The union must fight for a five hour work day and a four day work week. The profit level of industry is high enough to increase employment and end layoffs.

6. The union must fight for an immediate doubling of the wages of all production workers. Since 1960 wages of black workers have risen less than 25%. Yet profits have risen more than 90%. The pitifully small increase the black production workers have received has been completely wiped out by inflation. We know how wealthy the company is. We know how low their labor costs presently are. In fact, we know that it costs less than $100 in labor to produce a $3,000 car. We say increase that labor cost to $200 per car and double the wages immediately.

7. We demand a cut in union dues. The union already collects $10 million a month from its members and can't defend the rights of the workers.

8. We demand the end of the checkoff of union dues. While the check off was progressive in the 30's today it prevents workers from disciplining poor union leadership.

9. We demand that all U.A.W. investment funds be used to finance economic development in the black community under programs of self determination. The union now holds over $90,000,000 in strike funds in white banks. They lost over $1,000,000 in strike funds when a bank in California folded two years ago. We demand that all such money be held in black institutions and used in the black community.

10. We demand that the union end its collusion with the United Foundation. Black workers should contribute only to black controlled charities working for the benefit of the Black community, and that the $300,000 dollars in Peoples State Bank in Hamtramck be removed immediately and placed in Black Banks.

11. We demand that all monies expended for political campaigns by the U.A.W. be turned over to the Black United Front for Black controlled and directed political work.

12. We demand that the U.A.W. end its collusion with the C.I.A., the F.B.I. and all other white racist spy institutions.

13. We demand that the U.A.W. end all interference in the political, economic, social and cultural life of the Black community. That community and the Black workers in it are to exercise self determination in all political, economic, social and cultural activities and are to use black contributed union funds in any such activities. This means that the UAW end its affiliation with MDCDA, New Detroit, and other such programs and place all administration authority and funds in the hands of the Black community.

14. We demand an end to the harrassment of Black revolutionists and their leaders by the auto companies with U.A.W. Cooperation.

15. We demand that the U.A.W. use its political and strike powers to call a general strike to demand immediately:

    a. An end to the Vietnam war and withdrawal of all American troops.

    b. An immediate end to all taxes imposed upon workers.

    c. Increases in profit and industrial property taxes to make up the difference.

    d. Reallocation of all Federal monies spent on defense to meet the pressing needs of the Black and poor populations of America.

16. The U.A.W. must prevent retired workers from controlling in-plant union policies. In every U.A.W. election the Reuther machine buses in retired U.A.W. members, who are neither familiar with, or concerned about conditions inside the plants. These workers, the vast majority of them reactionary, anti-black, white racists, inevitably vote for reactionary, anti-black, white racist candidates who do not represent the Black workers in the plant. The U.A.W. must establish a special department for retired workers which related directly to the U.A.W. International in pressing their economic demands, so that they cannot hinder the struggle of rank and file workers inside the plants.

MICHAEL HAMLIN

THE BLACK MANIFESTO

May 1, 1969

We the black people assembled in Detroit, Michigan, for the National Black Economic Development Conference are fully aware that we have been forced to come together because racist white America has exploited our resources, our minds, our bodies, our labor. For centuries we have been forced to live as colonized people inside the United States, victimized by the most vicious racist system in the world. We have helped to build the most industrial country in the world.

We are therefore demanding of the white Christian churches and Jewish synagogues which are part and parcel of the system of capitalism that they begin to pay reparations to black people in this country. We are demanding $500,000,000 from the Christian white churches and the Jewish synagogues. This total comes to 15 dollars per nigger. This is a low estimate for we maintain there are probably more than 30,000,000 black people in this country. $15 a nigger is not a large sum of money and we know that the churches and synagogues have a tremendous wealth and its membership, white America, has profited and still exploits black people. We are also not unaware that the exploitation of colored peoples around the world is aided and abetted by the white Christian churches and synagogues. This demand for $500,000,000 is not an idle resolution or empty words. Fifteen dollars for every black brother and sister in the United States is only a beginning of the reparations due us as people who have been exploited and degraded, brutalized, killed and persecuted.

Underneath all of this exploitation, the racism of this country has produced a psychological effect upon us that we are beginning to shake off. We are no longer afraid to demand our full rights as a people in this decadent society.

We are demanding $500,000,000 to be spent in the following way:

1   We call for the establishment of a Southern land bank to help our brothers and sisters who have to leave their land because of racist pressure for people who want to establish cooperative farms, but who have no funds. We have seen too many farmers evicted from their homes because they have dared to defy the white racism of this country. We need money for land. We must fight for massive sums of money for this Southern Land Bank. We call for $200,000,000 to implement this program.

2   We call for the establishment of four major publishing and printing industries in the United States to be funded with ten million dollars each. These publishing houses are to be located in Detroit, Atlanta, Los Angeles, and New York. They will help to generate capital for further cooperative investments in the black community, provide jobs and an alternative to the white-dominated and controlled printing field.

3   We call for the establishment of four of the most advanced scientific and futuristic audio-visual networks to be located in Detroit, Chicago, Cleveland and Washington, D.C. These TV networks will provide an alternative to the racist propaganda that fills the current television networks. Each of these TV networks will be funded by ten million dollars each.

4   We call for a research skills center which will provide research on the problems of black people. This center must be funded with no less than 30 million dollars.

5   We call for the establishment of a training center for the teaching of skills in community organization, photography, movie making, television making and repair, radio building and repair and all other skills

needed in communication. This training center shall be funded with no less than ten million dollars.

6   We recognize the role of the National Welfare Rights Organization and we intend to work with them. We call for ten million dollars to assist in the organization of welfare recipients. We want to organize the welfare workers in this country.

7   We call for $20,000,000 to establish a National Black Labor Strike and Defense Fund. This is necessary for the protection of black workers and their families who are fighting racist working conditions in this country.

8   We call for the establishment of the International Black Appeal (IBA). This International Black Appeal will be funded with no less than $20,000,000. The IBA is charged with producing more capital for the establishment of cooperative businesses in the United States and in Africa, our Motherland. The International Black Appeal is one of the most important demands that we are making for we know that it can generate and raise funds throughout the United States and help our African brothers. The IBA is charged with three functions and shall be headed by James Forman:

- Raising money for the program of the National Black Economic Development Conference.
- The development of cooperatives in African countries and support of African Liberation movements.
- Establishment of a Black Anti-Defamation League which will protect our African image.

9   We call for the establishment of a Black University to be funded with $130,000,000 to be located in the South. Negotiations are presently underway with a Southern university.

10 We demand that IFCO allocate all unused funds in the planning budget to implement the demands of this conference.

In order to win our demands we are aware that we will have to have massive support, therefore:

1 We call upon all black people throughout the United States to consider themselves as members of the National Black Economic Development Conference and to act in unity to help force the racist white Christian churches and Jewish synagogues to implement these demands.

2 We call upon all the concerned black people across the country to contact black workers, black women, black students and the black unemployed, community groups, welfare organizations, teacher organizations, church leaders and organizations explaining how these demands are vital to the black community of the U.S. Pressure by whatever means necessary should be applied to the white power structure of the racist white Christian churches and Jewish synagogues. All black people should act boldly in confronting our white oppressors and demanding this modest reparation of 15 dollars per black man.

3 Delegates and members of the National Black Economic Development Conference are urged to call press conferences in the cities and to attempt to get as many black organizations as possible to support the demands of the conference. The quick use of the press in the local areas will heighten the tension and these demands must be attempted to be won in a short period of time, although we are prepared for protracted and long range struggle.

4 We call for the total disruption of selected church-sponsored agencies operating anywhere in the U.S. and the world. Black workers, black women, black students and the black unemployed are encouraged to seize the offices, telephones and printing apparatus of all church-sponsored agencies and to hold these in trusteeship until our demands are met.

5 We call upon all delegates and members of the National Black Economic Development Conference to stage sit-in demonstrations at selected black and white churches. This is not to be interpreted as a continuation of the sit-in movement of the early sixties but we know that active confrontation inside white churches is possible and will strengthen the possibility of meeting our demands. Such confrontation can take the form of reading the Black Manifesto instead of a sermon or passing it out to church members. The principle of self-defense should be applied if attacked.

6 On May 4, 1969 or a date thereafter, depending upon local conditions, we call upon black people to commence the disruption of the racist churches and synagogues throughout the United Stated.

7 We call upon IFCO to serve as a central staff to coordinate the mandate of the conference and to reproduce and distribute en masse literature, leaflets, news items, press releases and other material.

8 We call upon all delegates to find within the white community those forces which will work under the leadership of blacks to implement these demands by whatever means necessary. By taking such actions, white Americans will demonstrate concretely that they are willing to fight the white skin privilege and the white supremacy and racism which has forced us as black people to make these demands.

9   We call upon all white Christians and Jews to practice patience, tolerance, understanding and nonviolence as they have encouraged, advised and demanded that we as black people should do throughout our entire enforced slavery in the United States. The true test of their faith and belief in the Cross and the words of the prophets will certainly be put to a test as we seek legitimate and extremely modest reparations for our role in developing the industrial base of the Western world through our slave labor. But we are no longer slaves, we are men and women, proud of our African heritage, determined to have our dignity.

10 We are so proud of our African heritage and realize concretely that our struggle is not only to make revolution in the United States, but to protect our brothers and sisters in Africa and to help them rid themselves of racism, capitalism, and imperialism by whatever means necessary, including armed struggle. We are and must be willing to fight the defamation of our African image wherever it rears its ugly head. We are therefore charging the Steering Committee to create a Black Anti-Defamation League to be funded by money raised from the International Black Appeal.

11 We fully recognize that revolution in the United States and Africa, our Motherland, is more than a one dimensional operation. It will require the total integration of the political, economic, and military components and therefore, we call upon all our brothers and sisters who have acquired training and expertise in the fields of engineering, electronics, research, community organization, physics, biology, chemistry, mathematics, medicine, military science and warfare to assist the National Black Economic Development Conference in the implementation of its program.

12 To implement these demands we must have a fearless leadership. We must have a leadership which is willing to battle the church establishment to implement these demands. To win our demands we will have to declare war on the white Christian churches and synagogues and this means we may have to fight the total government structure of this country. Let no one here think that these demands will be met by our mere stating them. For the sake of the churches and synagogues, we hope that they have the wisdom to understand that these demands are modest and reasonable. But if the white Christians and Jews are not willing to meet our demands through peace and good will, then we declare war and we are prepared to fight by whatever means necessary. We are, therefore, proposing the election of the following Steering Committee:

Lucius Walker	Mark Comfort
Renny Freeman	Earl Allen
Luke Tripp	Robert Brone
Howard Fuller	Vincent Harding
James Forman	Mike Hamlin
John Watson	Len Holt
Dan Aldridge	Peter Bernard
John Williams	Michael Wright
Ken Cockrel	Muhammed Kenyatta
Chuck Wooten	Mel Jackson
Fannie Lou Hamer	Howard Moore
Julian Bond	Harold Holmes

Brothers and sisters, we no longer are shuffling our feet and scratching our heads. We are tall, black and proud. And we say to the white Christian churches and Jewish synagogues, to the government of this country and to all the white racist imperialists who compose it, there is only one thing left that you can do to further degrade black people and that is to kill us. But we have been dying too long for this country. We have died in every war. We are dying in Vietnam today fighting the wrong enemy.

The new black man wants to live and to live means that we must not become static or merely believe in self-defense. We must boldly go out and attack the white Western world at its power centers. The white Christian churches are another form of government in this country, and they are used by the government of this country to exploit the people of Latin America, Asia and Africa, but the day is soon coming to an end. Therefore, brothers and sisters, the demands we make upon the white Christian churches and the Jewish synagogues are small demands. They represent 15 dollars per black person in these United States. We can legitimately demand this from the church power structure. We must demand more from the United States Government.

But to win our demands from the church, which is linked up with the United States Government, we must not forget that it will ultimately be by force and power that we will win.

We are not threatening the churches. We are saying that we know the churches came with the military might of the colonizers and have been sustained by the military might of the colonizers. Hence, if the churches in colonial territories were established by military might, we know deep within our hearts that we must be prepared to use force to get our demands. We are not saying that this is the road we want to take. It is not, but let us be very clear that we are not opposed to force and we are not opposed to violence. We were captured in Africa by violence. We were kept in bondage and political servitude and forced to work as slaves by the military machinery and the Christian church working hand in hand.

We recognize that in issuing this Manifesto we must prepare for a long range educational campaign in all communities of this country, but we know that the Christian churches have contributed to our oppression in white America. We do not intend to abuse our black brothers and sisters in black churches who have uncritically accepted Christianity. We want them to understand how the racist white Christian church with its hypocritical declarations and doctrines of brotherhood has abused our trust and faith. An attack on the religious beliefs of black people is not our major objective, even though we know that we were not Christians when we were brought to this country, but that Christianity was used to help enslave us. Our objective in issuing this Manifesto is to force the racist white Christian church to begin the payment of reparations which are due to all black people, not only by the Church but also by private business and the U.S. Government. We see this focus on the Christian church as an effort around which all black people can unite.

Our demands are negotiable, but they cannot be minimized, they can only be increased and the Church is asked to come up with larger sums of money than we are asking.

Our slogans are:

ALL ROADS MUST LEAD TO REVOLUTION
UNITED WITH WHOMEVER YOU CAN UNITE
NEUTRALIZE WHEREVER POSSIBLE
FIGHT OUR ENEMIES RELENTLESSLY
VICTORY TO THE PEOPLE
LIFE AND GOOD HEALTH TO MANKIND
RESISTANCE TO DOMINATION BY THE WHITE
CHRISTIAN CHURCHES AND THE JEWISH SYNAGOGUES
REVOLUTIONARY BLACK POWER
WE SHALL WIN WITHOUT A DOUBT

EXCERPTS BLACK WORKERS CONGRESS MANIFESTO

Excerpts from the
BLACK WORKERS CONGRESS MANIFESTO

Our Objectives:

1) Workers' control of their places of work--the factories, mines, fields, offices, transportation services and communication facilities--so that the exploitation of labor will cease and no person or corporation will get rich off the labor of another person, but all people will work for the collective benefit of humanity.

2) An elimination of all forms of racism and the right of self-determination for African people, Chicanos, Puerto Ricans, Asians and Indians who live in the United States and Puerto Rico.

3) The elimination of all forms of oppression of women in all phases of society, on the job and in the home.

4) The right of all people to express and develop their cultural heritage throughout the United States.

5) The right of all people to express and develop their cultural and religious views without fear of persecution.

6) A halt to the growing repression and increasing fascism of the United States, the militarization of the police, the arming of right wing forces and the repeal of all repressive legislation that abolishes the right of people to assemble, to speak freely, to have privacy and to publish their political views.

7) The replacement of all class collaborators in the trade union movement with leadership that will fight for the international solidarity of all oppressed people, a leadership that will fight all manifestations of racism, white skin privilege, capitalism, and imperialism (the sending of money, armed forces and Christian missionaries from one country to another for the purpose of exploiting and oppressing its workers). This leadership must demand real equality for women in employment.

From Michele Gibbs Collection.

8) The creation in the labor movement of revolutionary Black caucuses, Chicano and Puerto Rican revolutionary caucuses, Third World labor alliances, independent revolutionary union movements and other forms of revolutionary labor association that will to break the strangle-hold of the reactionary labor bureaucrats and the capitalist class collaborators that help to prevent the working class people from understanding their historic role in controlling the means of production.

9) A twenty-hour work week where all the people of the United States will be employed and have the necessary funds for food, clothing, shelter and the right to improve their standard of living and enjoy the benefits of an industrialized society.

10) Thirty days of paid vacation time each year for all workers including women in the home and the use of all resort areas and the creation of new ones for working class people and the elimination of special privileges at resort areas for any group of people.

11) An elimination of speed-up, compulsory overtime, unsafe working conditions, inadequate medical facilities on the job, brutality and terror in the mines, factories and industrial plants of the United States and Puerto Rico.

BLACK WORKERS CONGRESS

(A full copy of the Draft Proposal: Manifesto of the International Black Workers Congress may be found in: Encyclopedia of Anti-Revisionism On-Line: *http://www.marxists.org/history/*)

DOWNTOWN DETROIT
RALLY AGAINST STRESS

Rally against STRESS. Black Workers Congress publication, 1971
From Michele Gibbs Collection.

MIKE HAMLIN RETIRES

By Charles E. Simmons
January, 2000

When veteran labor and human rights activist Mike Hamlin retired recently, hundreds of well-wishers turned out at Detroit's historic UAW Local 600 union hall to pay tribute to one of the Motor City's leading servants in a career dedicated to the struggle for social justice.

As a founding member 30 years ago of the Dodge Revolutionary Union Movement (DRUM), the Black Workers' Congress and the League of Revolutionary Black Workers, the son of Mississippi sharecroppers was a trailblazer in the battle against racism and sexism in the auto industry and also contributed to the building of bridges between workers and community organizations of various racial and ethnic groups. He forged unity between African Americans and organizations such as the Chicano-based La Raza in the United States southwestern states in their efforts to establish their legitimate and historical right to be in the U.S. And in Michigan, he supported the call of Chicanos and Puerto Ricans to oppose police brutality and to abolish the negative labels such as "wetbacks" and "illegal aliens". Hamlin gave support to and helped to promote the Puerto Rican call for their independence from the United States, an issue that has been forcefully resurrected recently as a human rights violation as a result of the U.S. Navy conducting frequent and live bombardment on inhabited land that belongs to the Caribbean nation.

The former Ecorse High School star athlete in basketball and football found common ground between African American and Arab factory workers in Dearborn and Detroit to dispel negative stereotypes surrounding religious practices and dress and to gain the support of Arab laborers in the struggle for workers' rights. As Hamlin recalls, "I was involved personally with Ishmael Ahmed and others in Dearborn when they first formed the civil rights group ACCESS."

Who would have predicted that the former U.S. Army Sergeant stationed in Korea and specializing in heavy artillery in the late 1950's would a decade later meet with ambassadors from Vietnam and Cuba and become one of the early leaders in America's greatest grassroots peace movement that would stop the U.S. bombing of Vietnam?

Who would have guessed that Sergeant Hamlin would pioneer in the call for the establishment of peaceful relations between Washington and Havana which···seven U.S. presidents later···still remains an ugly and festering sore in U.S. policy at the dawn of the new millennium?

Although as a returning veteran he was hired as a jumper on delivery trucks for the de facto segregated Detroit News in the early 1960's, a few years later, Hamlin along with General Baker and others was one of the founders of the revolutionary newspapers, the Inner City Voice (ICV) which championed the cause of rank and file workers against unfair labor practices. The bold and fearless paper staffed by students, workers and community activists called for an end to all forms of discrimination throughout Detroit activists, called for an end to all forms of discrimination throughout Detroit and the surrounding communities where the workers resided. In case it has been forgotten by elders or never known by younger readers, it must be pointed out that in the 1950s and 1960s African-American Detroiters suffered daily injustices of discrimination in housing, education, healthcare, public facilities and public and private employment. There was openly abusive police brutality by a nearly all-white police force. Detroit had a segregated Fire Department and civil service and Blacks had little or no political representation at the local, state and national level. The Inner City Voice also opposed U.S. policies of promoting international racism in the form of war and oppression abroad.

After graduation from Wayne State University with a Masters degree in Social Work with an emphasis of Community Organizing, Hamlin constructed new paths in the area of crisis management and conflict resolution and provided therapy for workers who suffered from the intense stress of the industrial environment. As he told the authors of the 1998 update of "Detroit I Do Mind Dying", "I'm the one they call in when there is violence in a factory---a shooting, a knifing or threats that neither management nor the union can deal with."

Indeed, during the recent retirement tributes at the Local 600 auditorium, one after another speaker recounted the tragic drama of Hamlin regularly rushing to the scene of emergency to talk with honesty and sensitivity to an embattled worker armed with a rifle or automatic weapon who had decided to take out his revenge against a system and bosses and to end his or her own life in the process. In varying degrees of conflict, these were among the thousands of troubled autoworkers and their families who Hamlin counseled during his last decade as a therapist. Some of these tragedies such as the multiple shootings at auto plants in Ford Rouge and Wixom made banner headlines but most of the thousands of confrontations and threats on the brink of life annually go unreported.

Examining the roots of the widespread and increasing workplace violence in the auto industry in particular and the nation as a whole, Hamlin points out that most of the major incidents involve white working class males who feel grievances against the employer or the system. A lot of them are connected with the militia or with people who are heavily involved with guns. Most often, says Hamlin, they are people who listen to and read right-wing material and people who do a lot of thinking about how they have been wronged, even though they may be making $100,000 dollars per year. "My view is that Rush Limbaugh is the greatest purveyor of hate in this country. I believe that whenever there is a shooting, the first question a reporter ought to ask is whether the shooter has been listening to Limbaugh. There are a lot of people filled with hate and especially against Blacks." Hamlin attributes much of this hate to the influence of the media, the politicians and the racist code words they use.

In a discussion about his current views on the 21st century challenges for labor and civil rights activists, Hamlin reflects on his four decades of experience working as a labor advocate and organizer. As he sees it, workers and people of color began this century with the ever present and intensifying problems of racism and sexism. Since Presidents Nixon and especially Reagan, "We've had a reversal of what we accomplished. There is now an attempt to completely reverse that progress and to take us back to where we were in the early sixties. With regards to sexism, women have taken one step backward and are about to take another step, especially Blacks and women of color whose gains were never equal to those of white women in the society as a whole and in the business community in particular. Another challenge, says Hamlin, is that the elitism that existed prior to the civil rights movement within the African-American community is now making a forceful comeback. "You see it in the fraternities and sororities and in some of the churches where the congregations see themselves as remote from the masses of people and have no sense of the notion that some Blacks are going to get ahead and separate themselves from the lower classes."

Regarding the persistent color line, Hamlin says, "The major problem is our own internal weakness from the standpoint of not having an organization to fight against racism and the racists. Without a grassroots organization with the proper leadership, we are basically impotent in this fight in the political and cultural arenas. In terms of the antidemocratic nature of our existing organizations and the decline of the mass movement, we have gone back to the old authoritarian leadership, the cult of the individual leader. The consequences are that the organizations are shortlived and the people gradually fall away from that type of leadership."

Hamlin argues that it is this lack of revolutionary organizations, leadership and coalitions that accounts for the ability of developers to grab neighborhood land throughout the city, for the lack of quality and community control of education, and for the continuation of discrimination and police brutality.

Addressing the changes currently taking place in Detroit, Hamlin observes that this is just the beginning of a turnaround. But he adds that "Many of the problems that we fought about in the 1960s and 1970s are worse such as police brutality. And the problem of corruption and the attitude among many police that they are not here to protect citizens but are here just to earn a paycheck continues to be a major problem. I read that the police solve about 30% of the murders. This is intolerable. And we know that one of the reasons the police in this community don't do a better job is that the people just don't trust them and for good reasons."

As Hamlin sees the problems and remedies for the African-American community in the 21st century, "You're nothing without a good organization and with a good organization the possibilities are unlimited. If we had something now like the League of Revolutionary Black Workers, we would be in action everywhere, major substantial and important action. We could surely stop these Uncle Toms from traveling from campus to campus spewing that backwardness and hatred that they carry on. But more important than that, we would be fighting for the rights of all people and building a coalition, and we have shown that that is possible. We showed that the working class could be mobilized and win battles. We were a left grassroots political organization based in the community which does not exist today. We showed we could build a coalition of workers, students, other minorities, women, whites and trade unionists. It required enormous energy, commitment and risk. My activities in the 1960s cost me two wives and lots of physical and health problems and that type of risk was common among civil rights activists."

Hamlin suggests that there are positive developments taking place in the current national union organizing that is underway by progressive members within the unions and the new leadership within the AFL-CIO. However, he also explains that the weakness is that progress is limited to trade union consciousness and issues but that is still an advance over where a lot of people are today. Another weakness says Hamlin, is the disproportionate power exercised by the skilled trades segment within the unions which tends to be increasingly conservative, racist, protectionist and systematically excludes minorities and women from their ranks. A recent positive example Hamlin points out is that AFL-CIO chair, Yokich has pulled a major coup by getting the corporations to agree to give the auto workers the Presidential Election Day off and that the election will have a major impact on national and state politics. What the unions need to do now is to increase their activities in the political arena and continue the fight against racism and sexism within the unions. Concerning the possibility of a third party, Hamlin supports the idea of the Labor Party now being formed but suggests that "It is a ways down the road before it can get off the ground and become an effective alternative."

When asked to name those who have contributed most to his growth, Hamlin attributes his development to his devoted mother and aunts in Mississippi who were very strong women. He also credits his development to reading such authors as Algerian psychiatrist Franz Fanon, the late president of Ghana and founder of the Organization of African Unity, Dr. Kwame Nkrumah, and Malcolm X. Now in his somewhat retirement as Vice-President of Value Options, Hamlin takes more time to enjoy his grandchildren and continues to take counseling assignments. He is currently re-reading another favorite author, James Baldwin who Hamlin praises for his social insight and independent thought in such books as "Another Country", "Nobody Knows My Name" and "The Price of the Ticket".

Summing up his experiences before he rushes off to offer counsel to yet another worker in distress, Mike Hamlin, husband, father and grandfather concludes, "Never before have there been so many Americans who ought to be natural political allies. This is a great time to be a revolutionary."

(Charles Simmons, J.D., was a member of the League of Revolutionary Black Workers and an international correspondent for "Mohammed Speaks" newspaper. He is currently on the Journalism faculty at Eastern Michigan University, on the Board of Directors of Detroiters Working for Environmental Justice, and a contributor to the "Michigan Citizen" newspaper.)

HAMLIN: U.C.L.A. SPEECH

The Black Workers Movement of the 1950's & 1960's Was Fueled by Rage

by Mike Hamlin

Text of a speech delivered by Mike Hamlin at a conference, "Rank and File Movements of the 1970s" which took place in the fall of 2005 at the Center for Social Theory and Comparative History at UCLA (University of California Los Angeles.

As I look at the plight of black workers today, it appears to me that we are very much in a time like the 1950's. If you piece together the unemployment rates, the poverty among young black people, police misconduct, New Orleans, Toledo, and you have broad contact with black workers, you see gathering clouds of the type that caused black workers to take up the struggle that brought on so much change in the 1960's and 1970's.

At this point in my life, rather than addressing the black rank and file movements of the 1970's, I feel that if I have anything important to say, it's about what happened in the 1950's and 1960's that brought black workers to the fore as a vanguard that electrified the black movement in calling for a revolution led by black workers. My paper will address these two decades from the standpoint of a revolutionary in the center of that storm.

The 1950's

The aftermath of World War II was a time of great change in the world. The war itself and the experience of blacks in it and with it was the beginning. Most of us were in the south at the outset of the war and had no real grasp of anything beyond the horizon. At the time, I lived in the primitive conditions of rural Mississippi which I consider the biblical hell. The "Willie Lynch Model" was working perfectly after 250 years and we all knew our place during "these good old days". Blacks were saying the "Pledge of Allegiance", singing "America the Beautiful", saluting the flag, and singing about the land of the "free" and the home of the brave.

Experiencing the war and then returning to the racist world back here was the beginning of understanding the true reality of this country. The reality being that America is a fraud and a lie. There is no greater lie or fraud in the history of the world. Conferences such as this should stipulate this at the start. So in the fifties, for the first time in history, we as young black men began the process of understanding where we were and what a monstrous crime America has perpetrated on us. It is useful, I think, to look at the factors that brought us to a revolutionary stance that said we were unable to live in the same old way.

First, there was the well-known experience of black soldiers who were treated like human beings in foreign countries while being subjected to racist outrages by Trent Lott and Orrin Hatch types back home. This was a major factor in the building of the consciousness of the black masses.

In this period, we moved from the south to the north and began to be exposed to a better level of education. As a person who came from share-cropping Mississippi, I became an avid reader and like many blacks in that time,

I studied everything that I could get my hands on that was relevant to our plight. A series of events during that period are important in understanding the black workers movement:

1   The Korean War in which blacks begin to question why are we killing these colored people and our-selves, and for what?

2   The rising tide of independent nations in particular China, Ghana, Guinea, Algeria, Kenya, Vietnam, Congo and Cuba. Many of the leaders of these coun-tries published ideas that we would embrace. Partic-ularly important were Mao, Nkrumah, Toure, Lumumba and Nyere. At some point it became clear that America was such a fraud that anything anti-American was probably good for us.

3   We began to study black history and American history and learned that slavery in the U.S. dwarfs any other crime against humanity in world history, and the people who benefited from this horrendous crime were still raping, murdering, oppressing and exploiting us at the time.

4   A series of events occurred that furthered the con-sciousness of blacks. Specifically, I am talking about Brown vs. The Board of Education, Emmett Till, Lit-tle Rock, Montgomery, numerous lynchings, acts of police brutality and a brutal and protracted period of unemployment in the north from the end of the Ko-rean War until 1961.

5   Typically, we began to see that America was as racist through and through as it is today but it was impos-sible to identify the racists. The U.S. has always hat-ed blacks but has kept it hidden. What we didn't know was that everybody was in on it. The scholars, teachers, ministers, and politicians were saying

"America is the Greatest Country in the World", the land of the free and the home of the brave. As Jimmy Durante would say, "What do we know?"

6   During this period, a flowering of culture occurred that contributed to the break-down of the shackles on black minds. There was the beatnik influence which raised questions of whether this life was worth living. There was the publication of the Invisible Man, Jet magazine, and the emergence of black authors and artists, especially poets who spoke to the black conditions. Particularly important were James Baldwin and Leroy Jones. This was the breakout period of rhythm and blues and a time of Charlie Parker and Dizzy Gillespie.

7   In the north as previously stated, there was a protracted period of unemployment with black families forced to live in extended family situations with no safety net. White workers and unionized workers continued to enjoy a privileged position relative to blacks and enjoyed the situation. Many of our mothers in the north continued as they had in the south, working as household help, even in some working class white kitchens. The choices for young black working class males were hanging on with the family, joining the military (the choice that I made), crime, drugs or suicide.

The 1960's

By the end of the 1950's, young black working class intellectuals were bitter, enlightened and filled with rage. The task as we saw it at that point was to strike a blow as Malcolm would come later to state "by any means necessary". The beginning of this decade had seen an economic policy pursued by President John F. Kennedy that revived the U.S. economy. This resulted in an influx of black workers into industries in northern factories, especially the 'big-three' auto factories in Detroit. This also was a time of the "first negro" in most companies. I, in fact, was the 'third negro' hired at the Detroit News.

I think that expectations were that these changes would pacify what had become a significant concern of the establishment, a growing army of "angry black men". As a matter of fact, Time magazine had a cover with a young black man with a rifle and bandoliers of ammunition and a huge headline "*The Angry Black Man*".

Meanwhile our rage grew as we watched the brutality of the southern struggle, dealt with segregation, discrimination and brutal police tactics. In the south especially on into the 1970's, any white person represented a death threat over any black person. Added to the years of slavery was 100 years of Jim Crow and lynching. As a proletarian, the black worker has certain class tendencies. He is first and foremost not non-violent, which was very significant in those times. The southern struggle was primarily waged by agricultural and service workers, middle class and students. Northern industrial black workers more than any others, believed in racial, class and international solidarity with the people of the Third World, as well as in self defense.

Within this context, you found the black working-class intellectual looking for a way to strike a blow for the oppressed. Some workers thought about armed struggle, others thought about suicide, including 'revolutionary suicide". Huey Newton frequently talked about "revolutionary suicide". The point is that racism can endure for a long time but will ultimately bring forth a revolutionary response which is what we represented in DRUM and The League of Revolutionary Black Workers.

We understood that previous progressive movements had been led by white people and as such, were only going to go so far. They could be halted by repression and concessions that stopped short of providing freedom and justice for black people. The labor movement at this time had followed and still follows this pattern. It is under-standable that to confront this system over the issue of the eternal and continuing crime against humanity is to risk death. History shows that almost the entire popula-tion of whites in the United States will move to destroy blacks if they get too far out of place. (See Rosewood, see Tulsa, see contemporary Detroit, and see New Orleans). In their behalf, I understand that it is a lot to ask of whites to give their lives for the freedom of black people, although many did during the period of the 1960's. Amongst those were Mrs. Liuzzo, Schwermer and Good-man, and Reverand Bruce Klunder. Thousands of others also risked their lives facing the wrath of the racist southerners during the decade of the sixties.

Let us be clear, in America to fight for justice, a black person risks death. Rosa Parks risked death, so did Martin Luther King, the Little Rock students, the Freedom-Riders, the students who participated in the Sit-Ins, Robert Williams, Medger Evers, James Meredith, the list goes on. So understand, that the fight for justice in America can mean death, especially if you are leading the fight. So it was that in 1960, in Detroit, a small band of black intellectuals took up the fight. We knew to make this fight we had to be willing to die. We took in every-thing that we thought might be useful. We studied Marx, Lenin, Mao, Fidel, Che, Nkrumah, Fanon, as well as the Vietnamese and many others too numerous to mention. We especially identified with those engaged in armed struggle, including the Cubans and all the liberation movements of the Third World.

The labor movement in the U.S. has sold out the black worker and was blatantly practicing discrimination

itself with blacks being in the dirtiest and most dangerous jobs and absent completely from skilled trades and
union leadership. We had studied the history of the labor
movements especially as they treated black workers.
Likewise the left in the U.S, with the exception of The
Progressive Labor Party and the Socialist Workers Party,
which had been intimidated and driven into hiding by
McCarthy. The new left was taking the position that the
working class had no potential as a class conscious force.
James and Grace Boggs, along with the Black Panther
Party, maintained that the key to the revolutionary
struggle in the U.S. was unemployed youth. We argued
that the struggle in this country had to be led by black
workers at the point of production and our main slogan
was "Black Workers Take the Lead".

In the beginning, there was the coming together of
two groups who were enraged and wanted to strike a
blow at this racist and oppressive system. You also had
workers who wanted better jobs, working conditions and
an end to discrimination and racist treatment on the job.
Within this very oppressive environment, we formed the
Dodge Revolutionary Union Movement (DRUM) in 1968.
Over the course of our existence, we struck two Chrysler
plants, shutting them down with just the black workers.
We knew the risks involved and that only the most
determined fighters would be able to carry it through.
The other slogan of note was "UAW means You Ain't
White" which highlighted the fact that what was consid-
ered one of the best and most progressive unions had
settled into a comfortable accommodation with its racist
members, especially in skilled trades.

By the time our movement reached its end, we had
helped spread trade union and revolutionary consciousness from coast to coast and border to border. We organized caucuses in many unions. We organized independent

local unions and we trained persons who occupy positions in unions to this day. Part of what we did was to inspire people to go into the plants and become organizers. Unfortunately, the organization that was the vanguard did not survive for many reasons too numerous to go into in this short paper.

This period corresponded with the implementation of Nixon's very successful Southern Strategy, which is the dominant political force today. This strategy seeks to inflame and exacerbate the powerful racism in the majority of the white population in the United States and is a principle factor in American politics since Nixon. A similar strategy has been followed by the trade unions and it has worked. This particular strategy involved recruiting blacks who would "play ball" and were an alternative to militant workers. This was carried out with the support of the corporations. Many opportunists and "Uncle Tom's" were promoted in the unions as an alternative to "those guys", the militants. They also incorporated a new generation of young black people who had no black consciousness, no class consciousness, no rage, no desperation or the imagination that comes with having one's back to the wall.

The 1970's

I am not going to say too much about this period although I have had pretty broad contact with workers and major players in the EAP and substance abuse field, working with UAW-Ford especially. I have seen the development of joint programs and participated in a lot of work helping workers with problems that threaten their lives, livelihood and families. My opinion is that most trade union activity is centered in keeping the opposition at bay and staying in office.

In our area, the unions made fundamental mistakes when they allowed Reagan to wed workers to the concept with his implicit and explicit promise to deliver a powerful blow to the despised race. In the Greenberg study on Reagan Democrats from 1988, he describes the Reagan Democrats from Macomb County, Michigan as saying blacks are responsible for everything that has gone wrong in their life. This is especially ironic since Detroit is home to the UAW and the Teamsters World Headquarters. Yet Detroit is the poorest and most segregated city in this country. Every election is a referendum on race in the State of Michigan and blacks are the whipping boys. Rage is once again building and it is only a matter of time before the "fire next time".

READERS STUDY GUIDE

1   What, if anything, had you heard or read about the League of Revolutionary Black Workers before reading this book? Can you remember any talk about the League in your home, school, church, or work?

2   What lessons can be drawn from the experiences of black revolutionaries and activists in the 1960's and 1970's? Why do you think that the Detroit black workers movement is generally ignored in the dominant narratives of that period?

3   What do you think drove the leaders of the League to take the risks, do the hard work, and allocate resources to build and project a revolutionary black workers organization?

4   Why do you think Mike Hamlin said that during this period, revolutionary suicide was an attractive idea to some young black males?

5   What lessons can be drawn from the women's League experience as described by Hamlin and Gibbs?

6   What is the work history of the adults in your family? How has that work affected or shaped their outlook? Your own?

7   How would you assess the role currently played by established religion in your community? In American society in general?

8 In 1956, The Civil Rights Congress charged the U.S. Government with practicing genocide against the black population of the U.S, according to the U.N. definition. How would you characterize the structural position of black people in the USA today?

9 The U.S. has taken millions of lives throughout its history from the genocide of Native Americans to lives in the Middle East and Africa today. What will make it stop?

10 Is a revolution necessary to right the wrongs in this country or can essential change be accomplished by electoral politics?

11 Can we expect black and white workers to unite and lead all the other disenfranchised people to take power from the capitalist class in the U.S?

12 Does any segment of the working class have revolutionary potential today? Why or why not?

13 How has racism served to keep the capitalists in power in the U.S?

14 Assess the impact of white people being a demographic minority in the U.S. today.

15 What additional questions did the material in this book pose for you?